LEGACY OF THE GLADIATORS

ITALIAN AMERICANS IN SPORTS

LEGACY OF THE GLADIATORS

ITALIAN AMERICANS IN SPORTS

By
Nick Manzello

Ambassador Books, Inc.
Worcester • Massachusetts

The Publisher wishes to thank the following for their permission to use cover photos: The New York Yankees, University Photo/Graphics at Pennsylvania State University, and Peter Marciano.

Library of Congress Cataloging-in-Publication Data

  Manzello, Nick, 1937-
   Legacy of the Gladiators: Italian Americans in Sports / by Nick Manzello.
    p. cm.
   ISBN 1-929039-12-3
   1. Italian American athletes--Biography. I. Title: Italian Americans
  in sports. II. Title.
   GV697.A1 M278 2002
   796'.0l895'1073--dc21

                        2002011998

Published in the United States by Ambassador Books, Inc.
91 Prescott Street, Worcester, Massachusetts 01605
(800) 577-0909

Printed in Canada.
For current information about all titles from Ambassador Books, Inc.,
visit our website at: www.ambassadorbooks.com.

To the memory of
Antonio and Elizabeth Manzello
and to my wife Mary.

CONTENTS

FOREWORD

The idea for this book and for its title came during an evening I spent with Angelo Dundee, a man who knew and managed or trained more world boxing champions than any other person.

We were having supper at the Four Seasons Restaurant in Worcester, Massachusetts, before Sugar Ray Leonard's comeback fight with Kevin Howard at the Worcester Centrum. Dundee listed Sugar Ray as one of nine champions he supervised during their reign as champion.

Dundee was polishing off a plate of well-seasoned linguine with red clam sauce when he paused. "You know, there's something about eating linguine that gets me to thinking about all the great Italian boxers, the champions and the ones who came close to wearing the crown.

"And I always think of Rocky Marciano and what he meant to boxing and to the Italian people. He was the real Rocky. He was a proud Roman. He reminded me of the great Roman gladiators I read about when I was a kid."

Thus was born the title of this book.

Dundee, who spoke Italian fluently, often spoke his parents' language during our conversations. He also made a point of using some of the spirited quotes offered by the people of the sporting world he met and knew.

"One time Vince Lombardi told me: 'Give me eleven Rocky Marcianos and I'll never lose a football game.' I'll do him ten better. Give me one Marciano and I'll give you a world-champion fighter every time."

Of Carmen Basilio, another gladiator, whom he managed to the world welterweight and middleweight titles, Dundee said: "He had Italian blood through and through. He was in a class by himself, not only as a fighter but as a man."

Willie Pep, considered in most quarters as the best boxer pound-for-pound to ever lace on gloves, was built in the mold of a Dundee, in that he seldom spoke a sentence without giving a hint of his Italian heritage.

The author, left, with Angelo Dundee.

It was a balmy summer afternoon at the Eden Restaurant in Worcester when I was first introduced to Willie. He was in town doing a little promotional work for promoter Sam Silverman. Willie and I struck it off well from the start, and I began an early flurry of questions pertaining to his sometimes rocky boxing career. I asked Willie if he resented all the bad things written about him over the years. "No way," said the former featherweight champion. "In fact sometimes it's [publicity] the best thing that could happen to me. The one thing that I got in my favor is over 200 fights. They can never take that and the fact that I'm made of good Italian blood away from me."

Tim Cohane, a writer of more than a half dozen books and perhaps one of Vince Lombardi's better friends in the sporting world, liked to tell the story of how he and Vince often talked about Vince's heritage. "He was the proudest Italian I ever met. He often spoke of his heritage and of his immigrant mother and father," said Cohane.

Legacy of the Gladiators, then, is the story of Angelo Dundee, Rocky Marciano, Willie Pep, Joe DiMaggio, Yogi Berra, Eddie Arcaro, and many more champions who rose to the heights with both dignity and pride in their heritage. It is the story of men who battled not only opponents but for a tradition that was in their blood.

Italian people have made great contributions to American society in entertainment, music, art, politics, law, medicine, education, food and, as this book demonstrates, sports. I have tried to portray the greatest names in Italian-American sports history in all the major sports and some of the not so major ones. There is more to athletics than just success. Character, integrity, loyalty, friendship, total commitment, dedication, and pride are necessary for true greatness. The athletes in this book display those virtues in abundance.

The sources for this book were many and varied: interviews that I conducted as a writer for the *Worcester Telegram* and for my television and radio shows; as well as conversations I had with many well-known sports figures. I also witnessed some of the historic events that I wrote about. For example, I was present at Yankee Stadium in 1949 for Joe DiMaggio Day. Other material came from the sports information offices of colleges and professional organizations. I also consulted old newspapers and magazines and encyclopedias, as well as gleaning information from the internet. A list of acknowledgments is contained in an appendix on page 303.

BASEBALL

Italian Americans have supplied talent for the great American pastime nearly since its beginnings in 1846. "Buttercup" Dickerson, born Lewis Passano, was the first Italian American to play in the Major Leagues. He began his career in 1878 as the starting outfielder for Cincinnati. He was only nineteen at the time. A year later he led the National League in triples with a total of fourteen. On June 16, 1881, he became only the fifth player on record to go 6 for 6 at the plate. Over his seven-year career in the Majors, Dickerson obtained a lifetime batting average of .284, an impressive figure even by today's standards.

Little if anything is known about Dickerson's Italian heritage, and he no doubt preferred to keep it that way. An Italian surname during that period meant limits; it meant having to confine oneself to the harsh and unfair stereotypes projected by the majority of Americans. It would be several decades before an Italian American could speak his name aloud with pride.

Courtesy of the New York Yankees

H e's as famous an American and as big a hero as there has ever been. There is hardly a soul living today who has not heard of him. Even those who know nothing about baseball or could not care less, know about Joe DiMaggio.

From 1936 to 1951, he was the best player in baseball. A lot of people think he was the greatest of them all. In 1969, Major League Baseball's Centennial Year, he was voted by the fans as the all-time center fielder and greatest living player. In addition to his superior baseball skills, he was the epitome of the clean-cut all-American boy. He was a gentleman. He was a good sport.

In a 1947 World Series game against the Brooklyn Dodgers, Dodger left fielder Al Gionfriddo

DiMaggio

took a home run away from him in the last of the sixth inning that would have tied the ball game. While most mortals would have reacted with angry frustration, he merely did a slight kick of the dirt while rounding second base.

Every little boy in America wanted to be just like him. Country singer Bill Anderson recorded a song in the late 1960s called "Where Have All Our Heroes Gone?" In the lyrics Anderson says, "My heroes were people like Joe DiMaggio who proved that nice guys can finish first."

During the troubled and turbulent sixties when Americans were gloomy, cynical and sorely lacking in morale and spirit, the popular recording duo of Simon and Garfunkel wrote and recorded a song called "Mrs. Robinson." Part of the lyrics state, "Where have you gone Joe DiMaggio? A nation turns its lonely eyes to you. What's that you say Mrs. Robinson? Joltin' Joe has left and gone away."

As aware of Joe DiMaggio as much as anyone else were Italian Americans. There has never been a greater source of pride or inspiration to an ethnic group than the Yankee Clipper. He was looked upon with the utmost reverence in such predominantly Italian areas as Shrewsbury Street in Worcester, Massachusetts; the

North End of Boston; East Boston; and North Providence, Rhode Island. This, despite the fact that the majority of the people who lived in these areas were Boston Red Sox fans and despised Joe's New York Yankees.

To be sure, he was human and vulnerable like everyone else. He had a bitter contract dispute with the Yankees in 1942, the year after his record setting 56-game hitting streak—that is one record that may never be broken. Joe rightfully expected a good raise. Yet, New York general manager Ed Barrow actually wanted to cut Joe's contract by $2,500 supposedly because of World War II. It was the only time Joe ever received negative publicity from the Yankees.

DiMaggio crossing home plate as a San Francisco Seal.

When he was the toast of the nation in 1941, a popular song of that era paid him tribute but also kept him in proper perspective: "Who started baseball's famous streak that's got us all aglow? He's just a man and not a freak, Joltin' Joe DiMaggio."

He also had two disastrous marriages, the second to the famous sex goddess of the 1950s, Marilyn Monroe. Once when Marilyn returned from appearances in Korea, she said, "Joe, you never heard such cheering." "Yes, I have," he answered.

Despite the fact that they were divorced, Joe took care of the funeral arrangements when Marilyn died of a drug overdose in 1962.

Joe DiMaggio will always be thought of as a New Yorker, but the man who was never ejected

DiMaggio

Baseball Hall of Fame Library, Cooperstown, NY

Joe DiMaggio takes his classic cut.

from a game was born on November 25, 1914 in Martinez, California.

DiMaggio

Before joining the Yanks, Joe learned his baseball lessons well in the Pacific Coast League, playing for the San Francisco Seals. In 1933, Joe had a 61-game hitting streak, the longest hitting streak in professional baseball history. All the Major League scouts were interested in him, but in 1934, he seriously injured his knee and most scouts were scared off. In 1935, Joe was the Pacific Coast League Most Valuable Player, hitting .398 with 34 home runs and 154 RBIs. He learned a lot from his Seals manager, Lefty O'Doul, a great hitter himself in his time. Despite his 1934 injury, Yankee scouts Joe Divine and Bill Essick still recommended Joe to the Yanks. Essick, in his forceful report to owner Jacob Ruppert, was especially high on Joe. The Yankee scouts were impressed by his going 1 for 4 in a Seals exhibition game against

Satchel Paige—perhaps more of a reflection on Paige's great talent. Joe underwent an exhaustive physical examination for the Yankee brass, and his knee was pronounced strong and fit. Yankee farm director George Weiss wanted Joe, and against general manager Ed Barrow's wishes, Jake Ruppert prepared to obtain him. In November of 1934, the Yanks acquired Joe from the Seals for an amount between $25,000 and $50,000. The Seals got in return five players. Joe played with San Francisco in 1935 then joined the Yanks for spring training in 1936.

Many experts consider Joe to have been the best all-around baseball player in history. He excelled at every facet of the game. Joe was a sensational hitter for average and power, a splendid, graceful, ball-hawking center fielder, and a great thrower. He was a daring and alert base runner, a heads-up player who never missed a sign in his entire career, and a team leader. Joe was everything a manager could hope for. His favorite manager, Joe McCarthy, for whom DiMaggio played between 1936 and 1946, loved Joe as a player and a person.

"DiMaggio was the complete player," said McCarthy, who also remarked that Joe "was the best base runner I ever saw. He could've stolen 50 to 60 bases a year if I had let him."

Joe gave 100 percent effort every time he stepped on the playing field. He was the Yankees' team leader on clubs that won ten American League pennants and nine World Championships. Some of Joe's career statistics do not measure up to those of other greats, but one must remember when examining Joe's lifetime stats that he missed three seasons in the prime of his career because of military service (1943–45).

During the war, Ted Lyons of the White Sox pitched his first game on Guam for his Navy team against Joe's Army team. Joe belted a home run and afterwards Lyons said, "I left the country to get away from DiMaggio and here he is."

Joe was completely dedicated to his profession. He was constantly learning more about the game and improving himself as a player. Any teammate interested in becoming better could go to Joe and receive expert advice. Joe remained in the clubhouse long after a game was over while less gifted players were in a hurry to run along. Joe always kept himself in top physical shape and adhered to training rules. He was a most responsible athlete and felt responsibility to the Yanks, taking each loss as a personal failure.

Joltin' Joe simply had the most beautiful, classic, fluid batting swing the game of baseball has seen to date. He took a wide stance at the plate and because he had tremendously strong wrists he could wait until the last instant before swinging at a pitch. Joe had as sharp a batting eye as any player in history.

In 1936, Joe hit 29 home runs setting the Yankee club rookie record. His 132 runs scored and 15 triples that same year were both American League rookie records.

In July of 1937, Joe cracked fifteen home runs, then the most ever hit during the month of July in Major League Baseball. He hit a total of forty-six home runs in 1937, the most ever hit by a Yankee right-handed batter. Joe knocked in more than 100 runs in seven consecutive seasons from 1936 to 1942. On five occasions, he set a Major League record by hitting four or more extra

base hits in a game. The Yanks counted on Joe to be their number one power hitter during his career, a job of considerable difficulty since Joe had to whale away into Yankee Stadium's center field—a veritable "Death Valley"—for half of his games each year. Joe hit two home runs into the distant left center field Yankee Stadium bleachers—which in those days were over 457 feet from home plate. On April 21, 1948, he hit the first home run out of the old Griffith Stadium in Washington.

As mentioned earlier, in 1941, Joe hit safely in fifty-six consecutive games, a record that is still the most awesome record in baseball history. The game after his streak was snapped, Joe began a 16-game hitting streak. Thus, Joe hit in 72 out of 73 consec-

Courtesy of the New York Yankees

The most beautiful, fluid batting swing the game has seen to date.

utive games. His .381 batting average of 1939 is the second highest in Yankee history.

Joe was a rarity in that he was a power hitter who had bat control, striking out infrequently. He had nearly as many lifetime home runs (361) as strikeouts (369), a tremendous feat for a power hitter. He struck out just once every 18.48 at bats and homered once per 18.89 at bats. In that memorable 1941 season, Joe struck out only thirteen times in 541 times at bat. His lifetime on-base percentage of .398 is the seventh highest in Major League history for a center fielder.

In Joe's first Major League game, he had a triple and two singles. That same year, on June 24, 1936, Joe had two home runs in one inning. In a double

header on July 13, 1940, Joe had nine runs batted in. On September 10, 1950, Joe was the first player to hit three home runs in a game at Griffith Stadium in Washington, DC. He hit three home runs two other times in a game and twice hit for the batting cycle: a single, double, triple, and home run in one game.

The battles between Cleveland's Bob Feller, the great fast-ball pitcher, and Joe often highlighted Yankee-Indian contests of the late 1930s, 1940s and 1950s. Actually, Joe did quite well in his confrontations with Feller. It was Cleveland's Mel Harder who gave the Yankee Clipper the greatest difficulty at the plate.

Joe began his rookie season of 1936 in left field, then moved to center field midway through the season, and remained the Yanks center fielder until he retired following the 1951 season. Joe's gracefulness in center field gave an easy look to tough plays. He got an immediate jump on fly balls and never laced his catches with dramatics. In fact, Joe rarely left the ground; he was usually camped under a fly ball waiting for it to come down. Not only did Joe have great instincts in playing batted balls, he was also a smart center fielder who never threw to the wrong base. Joe was intelligent at positioning himself according to his pitcher, the batter, and the count. He was a studious center fielder and his memory and willingness to learn made him great. He was, indeed, gifted but he also worked at being great.

DiMaggio

Joe made many great catches in his career, but one of the most memorable came late in 1939 at Yankee Stadium. Detroit's Hank Greenberg sent a monumental blast high and some 460 feet into the spacious center field graveyard. Joe turned and moved as soon as the shot was launched. He raced with his back to the plate and had an idea as to where the ball would land. Right at the famed monuments, Joe caught the ball on the fly and those present agreed it was the most sensational catch ever seen. The man who was robbed, Greenberg, was at second base when the out was made and would have had a sure inside-the-park home run.

In 1936, Joe led the American League outfielders with 22 assists. In 1937, he led in putouts with 413. He set the pace in double plays with five in 1941, and in 1947, he led in fielding with a .997 mark that is the Yankee club record for center fielders.

Joe's most heroic season was 1949. In 1948 he had played with an extremely painful right heel spur injury, and he had heel surgery following the season. Joe missed the first 65 games in 1949 and there was serious concern that his career was finished. But almost miraculously, Joe woke up one morning in late June and walked without pain. He played his first 1949 game against the Giants in the annual Mayor's Trophy Game and pronounced himself fit. Joe made his first regular season appearance in a key series at Boston. With tremendous flair, Joe put on a rousing show, hitting four home runs and driving in nine runs in a three-game Yankee sweep of the Red Sox. Even Sox fans, ardent Yankee haters, cheered his remarkable performance.

For the remainder of the season, Joe was at his finest, hitting .346 with 14 home runs and 67 RBIs in only 272 at bats. But in September, Joe contracted pneumonia and was hospitalized. After his release he deemed himself ready for the season's final two games against Boston at Yankee Stadium. The Yanks had to win both games to win the pennant. Although Joe was terribly weak, he was willing to give it a try. On the next to last day of the season, "Joe DiMaggio Day" was held and Joe received many gifts. He told 69,551 stadium fans, "I want to thank my fans, my friends, my manager, Casey Stengel, my teammates; the game's fightingest bunch of guys that ever lived. And I want to thank the Good Lord for making me a Yankee." Then Joe went out and hit a crucial double in a Yankee rally, helping to win the game. The next day in the year's finale, Joe was so exhausted he had to come out of the game while Boston was batting in the ninth inning. The Yankees won the game and the pennant, as Joe gave his last ounce of energy in the effort.

An important part of the DiMaggio legend was the way he conducted himself. Not once in his Major League career was Joe ever ejected for protesting an umpire's decision. He never badmouthed anyone. He was not involved in fights on the field or feuds with other players. Joe would not allow himself to be dragged into any seamy situations, and he got along with his teammates and, except for the bitter contract dispute in 1942, the Yankee front

Courtesy of the New York Yankees

DiMaggio unleashes his power.

office. In fact, Yankee management in the Dan Topping era thought so much of Joe that he was on hand when Casey Stengel was named manager in October of 1948. There were false reports that Joe and Stengel were enemies; their relationship may have been strained, but it never affected the team's performance.

Joe's teammates were fond of him and held him in awe much as the average fan did. In 1941, shortly after Joe's 56-game hitting streak ended, his Yankee teammates organized a small party in Joe's honor. The players bought a sterling silver cigar humidor that was inscribed "Presented to Joe DiMaggio by his fellow players on the New York Yankees to express their admiration for his consecutive-game

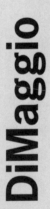

DiMaggio

hitting record, 1941." All of their names were engraved below the inscription. Joe, who had not realized how the team felt about him, was moved by the thoughtful gesture.

In 1949, Joe became baseball's first $100,000 player. He could have enjoyed the same type of salary for the remainder of his career, but he retired in 1952 rather than play below his standards. This pride and sense of fairness to the public contributed to Joe's bigger-than-life stature. After his comeback Boston series of 1949, Joe made the cover of *Life* magazine and was the country's biggest celebrity.

Joe won American League batting championships in 1939 and 1940. He was the league's home run champion in 1937 and 1948; the leader in RBIs in 1941 and 1948; and in slugging percent in 1937 and 1950. In 1937, he led the league in runs scored with 151.

Joe led the Yanks in many batting categories through the years, including: eight seasons in slugging percentage, and seven seasons each in hits, batting average, home runs, and RBIs. No Yankee has led the club more often in hits.

Joe's lifetime slugging average of .579 is the sixth highest in baseball history. In his Major League career, Joe averaged .89 RBIs per game, the fourth best average of all time. His 361 career home runs are the most ever hit by a right-handed batter in Yankee history.

Joe was selected to the American League All-Star Team every year of his career and played in a total of eleven All-Star games from 1936 to 1942 and from 1947 to 1950.

In 1936 Joe hit .346 in his first World Series. Joe's home run in the final game of the 1937 Series helped the Yanks eliminate the Giants 4-2.

In Game Three of the 1939 Series at Crosley Field in Cincinnati, Joe hit a long two-run homer putting the Yankees into the lead in an eventual New York win.

In Game Four of the 1939 Series, Joe scored the tying run in the ninth against the Reds. Then, with the score tied at 3-3 in the top of the tenth, the Yankees were at bat. Frank Crosetti was on second base and Charlie Keller on first. DiMaggio lined a single to left center field. The ball was misplayed by Reds center fielder Ivan Goodman and Crosetti scored. Keller raced home and collided with Reds' catcher Ernie Lombardi, who fell backwards and lost the ball. When Lombardi scrambled to pick up the loose ball, DiMaggio slid in behind Keller with the third run of the inning. The Yankees won the game 7-3 for a four-game sweep of the Series.

In the 1947 Series, Joe's home run won critical Game Five for the Yanks over Brooklyn 2-1. Joe's home run helped the Yanks win the final game of the 1949 Series against the Dodgers. In Game Two of the 1950 Series, Joe's tenth-inning home run into the upper deck of the left field stands at Philadelphia's Shibe Park beat the Phillies 2-1. After going hitless in the first three games of the 1951 Series, Joe's two-run, ninth inning home run clinched a 6-2 Yankee win over the Giants.

Joltin' Joe is among the lifetime leaders in many World Series batting categories. He ranks third in at bats (199); fourth in hits (54); fifth in runs scored (27), runs batted in (30), and total bases (84); seventh in home runs (8); and tenth in walks (19). Joe's eight home runs ties him with Bill Skowron and Frank Robinson for the most home runs by a right-handed batter in World Series history.

DiMaggio

Most observers felt 1951 would be Joe's last season and Joe himself realized he was slowing down when he started getting hits to right field, an indication that his bat was not as quick. On December 11, 1951, Joe officially announced his retirement as a baseball player. Through the years Joe went to Yankee spring training camps and served as a special instructor. He was often seen at the stadium and rarely missed an Old Timers' Day or special event, and, as always, Joe was accorded the honor of being introduced last.

From 1968 to 1969, Joe was the Executive Vice President/Coach of the Oakland A's and helped many young players, including Reggie Jackson. One of Joe's close friends, Edward Bennett Williams, bought the Baltimore Orioles in 1979 and invited Joe to get involved with the team. Joe became a member of the Orioles Board of Directors.

Joe was inducted into the Baseball Hall of Fame in 1955. The Baseball Writers named Joe the American League's Most Valuable Player in 1939, 1941, and 1947. *The Sporting News* also gave him their American League MVP Award in 1939 and 1941, besides picking him as the Major League Player of the Year in 1939. In 1941 the Associated Press named Joe the Male Athlete of the Year. In 1947 *Sport* magazine gave him the publication's first Champion of the Year Award, honoring his achievements on the field. *The Sporting News* selected Joe to their Major League All-Star team eight times, recognizing him as one of the three best outfielders in baseball. Joe won two other awards given by the Baseball Writers: the Sid Mercer Award in 1937 and 1941 and the Casey Stengel "You Could Look It Up" Award in 1974.

The Yankees retired his number in the form of a plaque, which was placed on the center field wall of Yankee Stadium and dedicated. In 1976, during Major League Baseball's celebration of the nation's Bicentennial, Joe's 56-game hitting streak of 1941 was voted the Most Memorable Moment in American League History. Joe is honored in the National Italian American Sports Hall of Fame in Elmwood Park, Illinois.

Joe DiMaggio often said, "The two greatest thrills I have received playing baseball for the Yankees were given to me by the fans."

After Joe was honored at Joe DiMaggio Day at Yankee Stadium in 1949, he said, "I cannot list all the gifts given to me, but they numbered in the hundreds. My mom and other family members were in attendance. Since we were playing the Red Sox my brother Dom was also present. I'd have to check the record books to tell you when I won the batting title. But I'll never have to check the book to tell

Courtesy of the New York Yankees

Joe DiMaggio is honored at Yankee Stadium.

DiMaggio

you about those 70,000 fans who came to Yankee Stadium to honor me.

"My other greatest thrill didn't happen at Yankee Stadium but at Fenway Park in Boston. It was Sunday, October 3, 1948, and a crowd of more than 30,000 had come to see the game; a big one for the Red Sox who needed a victory and a Cleveland defeat to tie for the league lead and force a playoff. My family was in the crowd and since we were out of the race and Dom's Red Sox needed the win, I know they were rooting for the Red Sox. The Red Sox fans were watching both the game and the scoreboard.

"After three innings, the Red Sox led 5-1 and Detroit was up 5-0 on Cleveland. I had a couple of big hits and we closed the gap to 5-4 in the fifth inning. The crowd was going wild. I had a charley horse in both legs and I could hardly walk. Manager Bucky Harris wanted to take me out of the game. In the ninth inning, Bucky sent Steve Souchock [as a pinch runner] in. I saw Souchock trotting toward first base to replace me. I was limping pretty bad as I headed for the Yankee dugout.

"I'll always remember what happened. The crowd was standing and roaring. I tipped my cap but the crowd continued to roar. I'll never forget looking into the stands and looking at the Boston fans giving an ovation to a guy who had tried to beat them.

"Following the game, I met with Dom and congratulated him on the Red Sox' 10-5 win. Dom was looking at me kind of funny, 'That was the greatest tribute a crowd here ever gave a ball player' said Dom. I told Dom that I bet he wanted to cut my throat when I hit one off the wall in the fifth inning. Dom said, 'No' and asked me to never tell Red Sox manager Joe McCarthy that he felt like applauding. I don't think that any player ever had a greater thrill than I did that day."

Since the Red Sox won that game and Cleveland loss to Detroit, the two teams met in a playoff game in Boston, which the Indians won.

On March 8, 1999, after a long illness, Joe DiMaggio died at age eighty-four in Florida.

Words of praise for the baseball legend came from throughout the country and some parts of the world, where the great one was loved and respected.

Then President Clinton, who was out of the country at the time, issued a statement on the death of DiMaggio. "I have no doubt that when future generations look back at the best of America in the twentieth century, they will think of the Yankee Clipper and all that he reached. Hillary and I extend our thoughts and prayers to his family," Clinton said.

Then Vice President Al Gore said: "In truth, Joe DiMaggio's famous hitting streak may have lasted

DiMaggio

fifty-six games, but for most Americans his memory will last forever, because we know that we will never see another one like him. Where Babe Ruth was known for his power and Jackie Robinson was known for his courage, Joe DiMaggio was known for his dignity and grace."

Dodger executive and former manager Tommy Lasorda had this to say about DiMaggio, "He was to people all over the world what a baseball player is supposed to be like. If you said to God, 'Create someone who was what a baseball player should be,' God would have created Joe DiMaggio . . . and he did."

Soon after the death of DiMaggio, news reached another Yankee great, Yogi Berra, who held a press conference in his home in Montclair, New Jersey.

"It's a sad day for baseball and everyone who knew Joe," said Berra, who was a teammate of DiMaggio's from 1947 to 1951. "When I think of Joe in the dressing room, it's always with a cup of coffee and a cigarette. He was a heavy smoker. He was a great baseball player and he always wanted to win. He was great on the field and off it."

Another Yankee teammate, Phil Rizzuto, while being interviewed on television by the author of this book, talked about

DiMaggio's great team influence, and about the way he changed the dress code of the team. "Before Joe became a Yankee most of the players would come to the game dressed casual and with shoes unshined. When he joined the Yankees he would be wearing a suit, clean shirt and tie. He would lay all his clothes down in order and the other players started taking notice of what Joe was all about. Soon after, most of the players started coming into the clubhouse dressed to kill."

Just how popular was Joe DiMaggio by the millions of fans who idolized him for what he was and what he brought to the game of baseball?

The famed bandleader Les Brown's recording of "Joltin' Joe DiMaggio" was a top hit of the day. The words: "He's in baseball's Hall of Fame, he got there blow by blow. Your kids will tell their kids his name Joltin' Joe DiMaggio. Joe, Joe DiMaggio, we want you on our side."

Even the great Ernest Hemingway, in his novel *The Old Man and the Sea,* made reference to Joe DiMaggio: " 'I would like to take the great DiMaggio fishing,' the old man said, 'they say his father was a fisherman. Maybe he was as poor as we are and would understand.' "

Joe DiMaggio was to baseball, what Michelangelo was to art and Luciano Pavarotti is to opera.

Courtesy of the New York Yankees

Berra

He was on the scene for two of the most famous, dramatic and exciting plays in baseball history.

The first was October 8, 1956, Game Five of the World Series at Yankee Stadium in New York. The New York Yankees were leading the Brooklyn Dodgers 2-0 with two outs in the top of the ninth. Pinch hitter Dale Mitchell was the last hope for the Dodgers. Those who heard the game on national radio were on the edge of their seats as they listened to the historic broadcast description: "Two strikes, ball one to Dale Mitchell. Listen to this crowd. Larsen checks the sign, here comes the pitch, strike three! A no-hitter, a perfect game for Don Larsen!"

Those watching on television and those who later

saw film clips of the game, witnessed the short, stocky catcher, wearing number 8, dive into Don Larsen's arms. It was the only no-hitter and perfect game in World Series history.

Four years and five days later, the same Yankee was on hand to witness another dramatic conclusion to a World Series, only this time his team did not come out on top. On October 13, 1960, Game Seven of the World Series with the score tied 9-9 in the last of the ninth, Bill Mazeroski led off for the Pittsburgh Pirates. The national radio audience was jolted by another shot heard 'round the world: "Ditmar throws. There's a swing and a high fly ball going deep to left, this may do it! Back to the wall goes Berra. It is over the fence, home run, the Pirates win!"

On the slow motion film, you see the ivy covered left field wall of the old Forbes Field in Pittsburgh, the baseball gliding over it and the left fielder in the New York uniform running toward the wall, his number 8 standing out like it did in the Larsen no-hitter. When the ball clears the fence, he quickly circles around and heads toward the dugout, no doubt dejected because he was a winner and winners hate to lose.

Only an outstanding, front line, versatile ballplayer could have been at those two positions at those two times in those two games. He is known for being an exceptional clutch hitter and an intriguing phrase-maker. He was the one who reminded us, "It ain't over 'til it's over."

His name is Lawrence Peter Berra, know to millions as "Yogi," nicknamed by his childhood friends after a movie character. From 1949 to 1963 he was one of the best, if not the best catcher in baseball and was also a very good outfielder.

He grew up a poor kid in the Italian section of St. Louis known as "The Hill," playing ball as often as possible with his buddies, including former St. Louis Cardinal and Chicago Cub catcher and later NBC sportscaster, Joe Garagiola. When Yogi came of professional baseball age, both hometown St. Louis clubs, the Browns and Cardinals, blew chances to sign him.

The Browns, perennial cellar-dwellers in the American League, felt he lacked ability, and the Cardinals' Branch Rickey, who gave Garagiola a $500 signing bonus, refused to give Yogi the same. Rickey felt Yogi was too slow and awkward to invest much money in him and told him, "You'll never be a ballplayer. Take my advice, and forget about baseball. Get into some other kind of business." There are some who believe that Rickey gambled and

Courtesy of the New York Yankees

Berra strikes a familiar pose.

lost; that he knew that he was about to join the Dodgers and wanted Yogi for Brooklyn. But most baseball people feel Rickey had too much integrity for such a maneuver. As great a baseball man as Rickey was, he made a major mistake on Yogi.

After being snubbed by the St. Louis teams, a frustrated Yogi went to work pulling tacks at a shoe factory. But Leo Browne, head of the American Legion baseball program in St. Louis, was convinced of Yogi's ability and contacted George Weiss, then the New York Yankees' farm director. Weiss sent Yankee coach Johnny Schulte to check out Yogi and without seeing him play, Schulte signed him to a $90 a month salary along with a $500 signing bonus. Schulte was willing to sign Yogi after receiving great scouting reports

Berra

from everyone he asked about the youngster. Just before leaving for his first minor league spring training camp in 1943, Yogi received a telegram from Brooklyn GM Branch Rickey asking him to report to the Dodger camp where he would receive a contract and a bonus. But by then it was too late.

After playing for the Yanks' Norfolk farm club of the Piedmont League, Yogi enlisted in the Navy in 1944 and saw D-Day action. Yogi was discharged from the Navy in 1946 and reported to the Yanks' Newark club of the International League. He had a great season, hitting .314 with fifteen home runs in only 277 at bats. The Yanks called up the 21-year-old late in the 1946 season and Yogi hit .364 in the season's final days. Yogi was one of the few rookies who knew the thrill of hitting a home run in his first major league at bat. It came off the Philadelphia Athletics' Jesse Flores and from his box at Yankee Stadium, New York general manager Larry MacPhail was heard to shout, "And Mel Ott wanted me to sell him for $50,000." The New York Giants had made an attempt to purchase Yogi when he was in the minors.

From 1946 to 1948, Yogi played about two thirds of his games as a catcher and the remaining third in the outfield. From 1949 to 1963, his final season with the Yanks, he was a catcher, left fielder and pinch hitter. After Berra was fired from his job as Yankee manager in 1964, he moved across the East River to Queens, to join his old manager Casey Stengel, then the pilot of the New York Mets, to play four games in 1965 and officially close out his playing career.

In his first two seasons he was not a top-notch defensive catcher. When Casey Stengel became the manager of New York in 1949, he had the immortal Bill Dickey teach Yogi the art of catching. Yogi worked hard to make himself a great defensive catcher with many hours of help from Dickey.

Yogi became a great catcher by learning all aspects of the position. In his first few years, Stengel or coach Jim Turner called the pitches. But by 1952, Yogi was calling the signals and outsmarting the hitters. He caught three no-hitters—two by Allie Reynolds in 1951 and the famous perfect game by Don Larsen in the 1956 World Series. Both pitchers credited Yogi for calling the no-hitters. In 1951, Yogi made 25 double plays as a catcher, the most in Yankee history by a catcher and the fourth highest total in baseball history. From July 28, 1957 to May 10, 1959, Yogi set a Major League record by catching 148 consecutive games without an error, handling a record 950 chances. Eight times Yogi led American League catchers in most games and most chances accepted, both league records. He led catchers in double plays six times, another American League record. Yogi ranks second on the all-time list in double plays for catchers with 175, fifth in all-time total putouts and chances from behind the plate, seventh in all-time games caught and is only one of four catchers ever to have a perfect 1.000 fielding percentage, having done that in 1958.

Yogi, a great athlete, was a surprisingly good defensive outfielder, especially late in his career. He played a fine left field. In September of 1961, the Yanks and the second-place Detroit tigers played a crucial series which the Tigers needed to win to remain in the pennant race. Yogi made a miraculous catch to rob Al Kaline of an extra-base hit to left field, and the Tigers' hopes died.

Berra

Many baseball experts and fans felt Yogi was the best player of the 1950s. Famous manager Paul Richards once said, "Berra is the toughest man in baseball when the game is up for grabs. He is by far the toughest man in the league in the last three innings."

Before the start of the 1960 World Series, Pittsburgh Pirate manager Danny Murtaugh observed, "Sure, the Yankees have some big bats in Mantle, Skowron and Howard. But the man we'll worry about most is Yogi Berra."

Early in his career, Yogi ducked out of an occasional game when he was tired and was scolded once by Yankee veterans who let him know that the team needed him. From then on Yogi was a tireless player.

Baseball Hall of Fame Library, Cooperstown, NY and Fred Roe

Berra at bat.

During the 1950s he caught more than 115 games in every season except 1958 and it was almost impossible to get him to take a day off. He knew the team needed him behind the plate, and being the heart of the team, Yogi was dependable. Even late in his career, Yogi worked long hard hours. Although he caught only thirty-one games in 1962 at the age of thirty-seven, he caught the entire twenty-two innings of the famous June 24 marathon game against the Tigers that took seven hours to complete, an American League record. Until that contest, Yogi had not caught a game all season. He was a ballplayer's player and an innovative one, too. He was the first catcher to begin the trend of leaving the index finger outside of the mitt.

As the unofficial captain of the Yanks during the 1950s, Yogi took much of the responsibility for the Yankees' pitching success. He treated each pitcher differently—some he goaded, some he babied. And Yogi was very protective of young pitchers. After his passed ball in Game Three of the 1952 World series, allowing two runs to score in a tough Yankee loss, Yogi protected his young pitcher, Tom Gorman, who had appeared to throw a pitch not signaled for. Berra told the press, "Gorman didn't do nothing wrong. He didn't cross me up, and don't none of you guys believe him if he said he did. I messed up the play. Blame me, not him."

The following spring Gorman said of Yogi's support, "It was the most generous thing anyone ever did for me. Up until now, no one would believe me—including Casey. Yogi told him not to listen to me. But I knew what he was doing. He was trying to protect a young kid like me from being branded a goat, as unselfish an act as I've ever experienced. I crossed him up. The blame was mine, not Yogi's."

Yogi hit thirty home runs in 1952 and 1956, the most ever hit by a catcher in the American League. In seven consecutive seasons, Berra led New York in runs batted in. Three times he led the club in at bats, doubles, and home runs. Twice he led in games played, runs, hits and slugging percentage. His 313 career home runs is the all-time American League record for catchers. Yogi was one of the greatest clutch hitters of all time and along with Roberto Clemente, was probably the best bad ball hitter in history. He swung at anything that looked good to him because he was so aggressive at the plate. Fred Hutchinson once remarked, "Yogi's a bad ball hitter, all right. But don't ever throw him a good one."

Yogi was at his best when it counted most, down the pennant stretch and in the World Series. He was a leader, a clutch hitter and a source of strength when things got sticky in the heat of a big game. Yogi was recognized around baseball during his era as the man most likely to respond favorably in a pressure situation, and he was involved in many. He

Berra

Courtesy of the New York Yankees

Mickey Mantle greets Berra after a home run.

played on ten World Championship teams. No one else in baseball history can say as much.

There is no question that Yogi was one of the most popular people ever to wear a baseball uniform, and he has been a national celebrity for almost thirty-five years. Yogi says things that sound funny and Yankee fans and all of America have enjoyed his remarks, known as "Yogi-isms." On Bill Dickey's tutoring, Yogi replied, "Dickey is learning me his experiences." Before a "Yogi Berra Night" crowd in St. Louis he said, "I want to thank everyone for making this night necessary." Casey Stengel greatly respected Yogi, often saying he felt of all those he ever managed, only Joe DiMaggio was a better player. Stengel

said, "To me he is a great man. I am lucky to have him and so are my pitchers. He springs on a bunt like it was another dollar."

Yogi is among the top ten in most Yankee career batting categories. His eight pinch hit home runs tie him with Bob Cerv for the most ever hit by a Yankee.

From 1948 to 1962, Yogi was selected to the American League All-Star Team. He hit a home run in the 1959 game.

Berra played in fourteen World Series, more than anyone else in history. He is first in total World Series games played with 75, has the most at bats with 275, most hits with 71, most doubles at ten and is among the leaders in many other categories. In 1947 he had the first pinch hit home run in Series history. He hit at least one home run in nine World Series, a record he holds with Mickey Mantle. Other Series records Berra holds are knocking in at least one run in eleven Series, scoring at least one run in twelve Series, walking at least once in thirteen Series and throwing out thirty-six attempted base stealers in Series play.

Yogi was a player-coach for the Yankees in 1963 and retired as a player following the season. He was named manager for the 1964 season and guided the Yanks to the American League Pennant, their final one in that era as the greatest dynasty in baseball. They would not win another until 1976. After the Yanks lost the World Series in seven games to the St. Louis Cardinals, Berra was dismissed. He joined the New York Mets in 1965 as a coach for Casey Stengel and was even put on the roster to play four games. He remained as a coach for the Mets until 1971 and was the Mets' manager from 1972 to 1975, winning the National League Pennant in 1973, making him only one of three men to have managed pennant winners in both leagues.

Yogi returned to the Yankees as a coach in 1976 and was named manager for the 1985 season. However, after a slow Yankee start, only sixteen games into the season, volatile owner George Steinbrenner saw reason to dismiss Berra and replace

Berra

him with Billy Martin. But Yogi has been as much a part of Yankee tradition as anyone who has ever worn the pin stripes. As a player-coach-manager, Yogi has been a member of eighteen Yankee pennant-winning teams and twelve World Championship clubs.

Berra has received many honors, among them: being inducted into the Baseball Hall of Fame in 1972, being named as the American League's Most Valuable Player by the Baseball Writers three times, being named to the *Sporting News'* Major League All-Star team five times and being named the best catcher in 1957, receiving the Top Professional Athlete Award in New Jersey by the New York Athletic Club in 1954. Also in 1954, he was named "The Top Professional Athlete" of the New York Metropolitan area by the New York Chapter of B'nai B'rith. And he is, of course, honored as a member of the National Italian American Sports Hall of Fame.

Rizzuto

S ometimes even the most knowledgeable people in sports make dumb mistakes. Take Casey Stengel for example. After Phil Rizzuto graduated from high school in 1936, Stengel, who was employed by the Brooklyn Dodgers at the time, refused to sign Rizzuto. Stengel told the future Hall of Fame ball player that he was just too small.

Not many others made the same mistake, however. Four years later, in 1940, *The Sporting News* named Phil Rizzuto the Minor League Player of the Year for Phil's outstanding play at the Yankees' Kansas City farm team. With the Yanks in 1941, Phil was Rookie of the League (before the official rookie awards as we know them today were given out).

He also won the Catholic Youth Organization's Most Popular Yankee Award.

In 1950, the Baseball Writers selected Phil as the MVP of the American League. The same year *The Sporting News* picked him as the Major League Player of the Year. In 1950, Phil also won the first Hickok Belt Award as the Top Professional Athlete of the Year. For four years in a row (1949–52), *The Sporting News* named him to their Major League All-Star team as the best shortstop in baseball. Phil was selected to the American League All-Star team five times, 1942 and 1950 to 1953. In 1981, Phil was presented with the Pride of the Yankees Award, given each year by the Yankee Foundation.

Following his 1936 graduation from Brooklyn's Richmond Hill High School, he not only failed to hook up with the Dodgers, the Giants also said he was too small. Yankee scout Paul Krichell saw Phil play a semi-pro game at Floral Park on Long Island and was impressed, so he invited him to a Yankee Stadium tryout. After several days of workouts, and several more days of anxious waiting, Krichell signed Phil—almost waiting too long and allowing the Red Sox to sign him. Yankee general manager Ed Barrow once said of Phil's signing, "Rizzuto cost me fifteen cents, ten for postage and five for a cup of coffee we gave him the last day he worked out at the stadium."

Phil began playing in the Yank's farm system for about $75 a month in 1936, playing in Bassett, Virginia, where his career almost came to an end. A leg injury, incurred when he stepped in a gopher hole, became infected and gangrene set in. For a time, Phil was threatened with the loss of the leg. Later he played in Norfolk, Virginia, and in 1939 went to Kansas City. Under Norfolk manager Ray White, Phil hit .336 (1940) against topnotch minor league pitching. Billy Hitchcock, a Kansas City teammate, nicknamed Phil "Scooter." Phil teamed with Jerry Priddy to form the best double play combo in minor league history. Both were invited to the Yankees' 1941 spring camp and both made the big

Rizzuto

league club. By the time Phil's minor league days were over, he had proved the Dodgers and Giants terribly wrong—not about his size, but about his ability.

Phil was the greatest shortstop in Yankee history. As a rookie in 1941, he was the Yanks' regular shortstop and hit a robust .307. He was Yankee shortstop every year from 1941 to 1954, except for his years of Navy service (1943–45). From 1955 to 1956, he was a Yankee, but played less than regularly.

Baseball Hall of Fame Library, Cooperstown, NY

Rizzuto turns the double play.

Rizzuto

In August of 1942, Phil enlisted in the Navy. He was given a leave of absence until October 6, allowing him to finish the 1942 baseball season. The Cardinals beat the Yanks in Game Five to wrap up the World Series on October 5. If a Game Six had been necessary, Phil would have been unable to play.

In the Navy, Phil contracted malaria and the sickness continued to plague him during the first three seasons upon his return to the Yankees (1946–48).

Phil was a key member of nine Yankee pennant-winning teams and seven World Champions; some would say he was the backbone of those great teams. Joe McCarthy once said of him, "For a little fellow to beat a big fellow he has to be terrific, he has to have everything, and Rizzuto's got it."

Phil brought that talent and determination to the Yanks. In 1949, Tommy Henrich, who had suffered a broken toe after chasing a foul ball and slipped into the Yankee dugout, said from his hospital bed, "We have nothing to worry about as long as Rizzuto remains healthy. He's the team's spark plug."

Late in the 1949 campaign, Boston's Ted Williams pointed to Phil and told Henrich, "If we had that little squirt, we'd be out in front by ten games now."

In 1950, Phil set a club record for Yankee shortstops by getting 200 hits in a single season. Besides being a fine hitter, he was a great defensive player, and he did all the things characteristic of a smart, heads-up player. He was durable, had good speed, and may have been the best base runner of his era. He was one of the game's greatest bunters. In 1951, Ty Cobb said that two players, Phil and Stan Musial, were the only mid-century players who Cobb felt would have been stars in his time. Cobb pointed to Phil's ability to hit to any field, to his great bunting skills, and his all-around defensive genius. Phil was a master at handling the bat. He led the Major Leagues in sacrifice hits four straight years (1949–52), a Major League record for most years and most consecutive years leading the Major Leagues. In 1947, Phil was hit by a pitched ball eight times, leading the American League.

Phil overcame many fears to play Major League baseball. He was terrified of flying. He was afraid of being on a baseball diamond (or anywhere else) during an electrical storm. He was frightened of snakes or anything that crawls. His fears were so apparent that teammates were naturally given to practical jokes. Phil was sometimes a willing victim—provided the joke did not involve a real crawler. He found so many unpleasant things tucked in his glove that he was one of the first players to bring his glove to the dugout between innings. The popular Phil somehow found a way to keep his active fears in check during his playing career. It should be added that Phil was fearless on the field, holding his ground as rugged runners barreled into second base.

Phil made the most important play of the 1951 season on September 17, a suicide squeeze bunt in the bottom of the ninth to score Joe DiMaggio and beat the Indians, 2-1, putting the Yanks into first place for the remainder of the season. After the game, an admiring Casey Stengel remarked, "Only Rizzuto could have bunted that ball successfully the way it was pitched, high and inside." The Indian pitcher, realizing that a squeeze was probably on, hurled the toughest possible pitch to Phil, but he still executed the play to perfection.

In another late season game in 1951, Cleveland's Jim Hegan blooped a fly between left field and the infield. Phil dashed into shallow left and with his back to the plate snatched the ball in the air with his bare hand. He stumbled, fell and rolled into foul territory, but Phil kept the ball in his bare hand for the out.

Phil was a marvelously graceful shortstop. Known for his acrobatics around second base, he worked brilliantly on the double play with five different regular Yankee second basemen (Joe Gordon, George Stirnweiss, Jerry Coleman, Billy Martin and Gil McDougald) in his Yankee career. Casey Stengel once said of Phil,

Rizzuto

"He is the greatest shortstop I have ever seen in my entire baseball career, and I have watched some beauties. Honus Wagner was a better hitter, sure, but I've seen this kid make plays Wagner never did. If I were a retired gentleman, I would follow the Yankees around just to see Rizzuto work those miracles every day."

In one streak, Phil accepted 238 straight chances without making an error. He led American League shortstops in fielding in consecutive seasons (1949 and 1950). Twice he led American League shortstops in double plays and putouts, and in 1952 he led American League shortstops in assists (458). Phil helped turn 123 double plays in 1950, setting a Yankee club record for shortstops. Phil ranks sixth on baseball's all-time shortstop double play list (1,217).

Courtesy of the New York Yankees

Rizzuto avoids a runner to make the throw to first.

Phil led the Yanks in stolen bases eight times, more often than any Yankee player in history except Mickey Mantle who tied him. Five times Phil led the Yanks in games played. He led the club in at bats three times. Twice he led the team in runs, hits, doubles and triples. In 1950 Phil led the Yanks in seven major offensive categories (runs, hits, doubles, walks, stolen bases, batting, and at bats).

In 1981 Willie Randolph passed Phil on the all-time Yankee stolen base list, leaving Phil in ninth place (149). Phil is also ranked ninth on the all-time Yankee games played list (1,661) and tenth on the Yanks' hit (1,588) and at bat (5,816) lists.

Phil ranks among the leaders in most lifetime World Series offensive categories. He is third in

Rizzuto

stolen bases (10) and fourth in walks (30) on those all-time Series lists. In the 1942 Series, Phil led both competing clubs in batting (.381) and hits (8). In Game Five of the 1942 Series, Phil's home run almost rallied the Yanks in a 4-2 loss to St. Louis. His two-run home run in Game 5 of the 1951 Series, helped rout the New York Giants, 13-1.

The Yanks released Phil in August of 1956, ending his tremendous thirteen-year Major League career with an abrupt stroke, although it was a most difficult decision for General Manager Weiss and Manager Stengel to make. Despite the August release, the Yankee players showed their feelings for Phil by voting him a full World Series paycheck.

In 1957, Scooter was hired as a Yankee TV-Radio broadcaster, joining Mel Allen and Red Barber. He held the job until 1995 and truly was the "Voice of the Yankees" once Allen departed in 1964. Phil began his association with the Yanks in 1941 (and the organization in 1936) and probably knows more about the club's last sixty years than anyone alive. Phil is loved by Yankee fans and is liked by nearly everyone in baseball, many of whom felt he should be in the Baseball Hall of Fame for his defensive brilliance alone. Finally, Phil has his rightful place. He was elected to the Baseball Hall of Fame in 1994. Holy Cow!

Rizzuto

Courtesy of the Los Angeles Dodgers

Campanella

A short, stumpy guy with stubby arms, hands and fingers; a soft tan covering a round face and big eyes filled with humor and inquisitiveness; love of fellow man and love for the game he played—that's Roy Campanella.

This rotund catcher who knelt in adoration, it seemed, every time he swung his powerful bat, his right knee skinning the ground as he picked up a low fast ball or curve, could put the ball over the infield, into right field or left, against any wall and over any barrier.

Campy was a complete player because he knew the game from the cradle on up—joining a professional outfit at fifteen years of age and catching games day after day, even four in one day at times, and seldom fewer than two per day.

Born of an Italian father, John Campanella, and a negro mother, Ida, Roy grew up in the Nicetown area of Philadelphia. His dad was a fruit and vegetable huckster who eventually owned a few stores. His mother instilled in him a love for God and the Bible and a warm feeling for all humans—lessons which Roy never forgot and always followed.

Borrowing his older brothers' baseball equipment, he played in neighborhood games and found out he had a powerful arm that lent itself to pitching. His high school coach tried Campy behind the plate and the young player told him, "If you want me behind the plate, then I need catcher's equipment, otherwise no catch." The coach knew that he had something special in an arm that could throw out base runners (a luxury at that level of kid's ball), and soon Roy had the equipment he wanted.

His reputation for catching and all that went with the trade caught the eye of a manager of the black pro clubs. At fifteen, not yet a senior in high school, after much cajoling of his mother, who needed assurance that Roy could go to church on Sundays, he joined the Baltimore Elite Giants. His dad, who wouldn't miss a game Roy caught, was easy to convince because he saw the massive drive Roy had to make good in baseball.

Campanella

In the Negro Leagues of that level, if you played you got paid, if you didn't play there was no pay. The Elites traveled all over the country playing about 200 games per year and Campy caught almost every one.

In his early days, Campy had a problem releasing the ball. He would take a bit of a windup before he threw. Biz Mackey, who should have gone into the Hall of Fame before a few who are in there now, was his manager. Mackey was a huge catcher who handled pitchers like little boys who needed direction. Biz took Roy under his wing and smoothed out his style. Later, Clyde Sukeforth of the Dodgers put the big league touch to it.

"I never knew what I was batting in those days," Campy said. "Most of our games were exhibitions, but since we got paid to play those just like league games, they were important to us. I could tell I was getting more sure of myself at bat, knowing I was getting on base more, hitting longer shots and batting higher in the lineup. During the winters I'd play in the Caribbean; in Cuba, Puerto Rico, Mexico, and the Dominican Republic.

"So I picked up more at bats than the law would allow. I got so used to seeing every kind of pitch, legal and illegal, righties and lefties, that I felt at home either in front or behind the plate."

Charley Dressen, then working for the Dodgers, set up an all-star game in 1945 between the pick of the blacks and minor leaguers of the Dodger system. After the game, Dressen told Campanella to see a man named Branch Rickey the next day.

Campy did not know who Rickey was or where he was, but he found the Dodger offices the next morning.

"Young man," the Orator of the Gowanus intoned, "would you like to play in Nashua for $170 a month?" Roy, who learned about dollars before he shaved, knew he was making better than $500 per month in the Negro League.

"Mr. Rickey, I'd have to think that over. I have to play winter ball in Cuba this next month," Roy said. Rickey popped in with, "Let me know when you are finished down there."

As Campy said, "I was having a cup of coffee and rolls later with Jackie Robinson and he spilled the beans about what Rickey was going to do. Boy, was I a dope! Jackie already was committed to sign and here I didn't understand what Rickey was telling me. That's how Jackie signed ahead of me."

As soon as the Cuban Winter League closed, Campy beat it back to the Cave of the Winds (Rickey's office) and prepared to ink a pact. In all his Machiavellian wisdom, the Mahatma signed Roy and sent him to Nashua, New Hampshire of the New England League, where racial prejudice was nonexistent, except for the hard lines that separated the Lowells and the Cabots from the MacCarthys

National Baseball Hall of Fame Library, Cooperstown, NY

Campanella goes after a foul ball.

Campanella

and the Giovannis, and that was measured mostly in dollars.

Walt Alston was his manager at Nashua and Don Newcombe was Campy's roommate. Alston, never a dummy, told the assembled squad that if he ever was bounced by an umpire, Roy would take over as manager. The white players on the squad took it in stride. Roy's first time as fill-in skipper worked out fine. With the game on the line, he sent up roomie Newcombe to pinch-hit. Newk, always a fine hitting pitcher, promptly unloaded a base-clearing homer that won the game.

The Dodgers moved Campy to Montreal in the Triple-A International League, where he joined the league as its best catcher. Rickey called him to the

Dodgers and pulled another of his sleight-of-hand tricks.

"Roy," said Branch, "I'm bringing you up as an outfielder."

"Mr. Rickey," Camp answered, "I know I'm colored, but I also know I am one damn fine catcher!" Rickey, who had the whole Dodger system to look after, didn't blink an eye.

"Roy," he said, "you are the best catcher on the Dodgers right now. However, I want you for a special purpose. I want you to go to St. Paul."

"St. Paul?" Campy asked. "Ain't that the same Triple-A level I left at Montreal?"

"Roy," the Mahatma said in a sepulchral, rising tone, "I want you to break the color line in the American Association!"

Campanella just shook his head. What had he gotten himself into? He was king of the Negro League catchers and could hit a ton and make more money than he would make rattling around in the minors.

What Rickey was doing was getting rid of the color barriers in all the top minor leagues so that he could place the many black players he planned on signing.

"Mr. Rickey," Roy finally said, "I'll go, but I don't plan on staying there too long." In two months, Campy was back on the Dodgers—as a catcher—and he never left.

What Roy accomplished as a hitter and catcher are etched in Cooperstown's Hall of Fame. He was Most Valuable Player three times (1951, 1953, 1955), led all catchers in homers in his time, nurtured a Brooklyn staff of flakes, flingers and fancy Dans to pennant after pennant.

How did he do it?

"My job as catcher was to know all my pitchers," Roy said, "what they threw, what they could throw *that* day, what they were feeling and what they were planning to do. I had to know my own manager's mind and what his plan was, the other manager and his plan, and what the other side's runners were planning. Of course, you have to know their hitters bet-

Campanella

ter than your own. Add to that knowing who I had to prod to produce, like Newk, or slow down like Billy Loes, or keep coming like Carl Erskine who pitched smart, all these things together make a catcher, who should be the manager's top advisor."

More than the mechanics and the technical know how, Campy was the team's father-confessor, the cap to Robinson's volcano, the soft approach to racial matters in contrast to the abrasiveness of the baseball militants. His balanced outlook was a gift from his teacher-like

In the on-deck circle.

mother. One incident bears it out.

As a youngster Roy hung around with his neighborhood mates who were all black. After they taunted him about his father, Roy came running home, almost in tears, and said to his mother, "Mom, is Daddy *really* white?" She put her hands on his shoulders and said to him, "Roy, baby, does it *really* matter?" This acceptance of humanity in all forms never left him.

Thus Roy could speak from many pulpits—he played in the segregated Negro Leagues; he was a color-barrier breaker for Rickey; he mastered the art of hitting and the art of throwing; and he had an unquenchable love of the game and never tired of playing it. For an Ernie Banks, who would say, "It's a great day for baseball. Let's play two." Campy would add, "Let's play three."

His ability to play hurt stemmed from his Negro ball days when it was no play, no pay. He earned fine money and asked for what he felt he deserved. He kept his family foremost in his heart. One time, when an explosion seared his eyes, he sat in his hospital bed and wondered: "How am I going to protect my family if my playing days end like this?"

As soon as the fog cleared, and he was back to normal, he approached Rickey for some added money to buy a liquor store. Roy mortgaged everything he could but needed extra money. Rickey, a teetotaler all his life, suggested a sporting goods company. Campy said, "Mr. Rickey, I'm colored and there aren't too many businesses I can go into. Too many accounts would be closed to me. But a liquor store has bottles and they are good as long as you have them. They don't go out of style, and I get the same bottle the snazziest hotel or night club gets."

Branch got up the scratch. When he sold out to Walter O'Malley, O'Malley took over where Branch left off. Roy, thus, had a business with steady income which served him in good stead while playing, and then it was there when he really needed it.

Campy balanced his base hits and RBIs. He batted high in the lineup, his pitchers performed as they should, and his salary climbed to heights undreamed of years earlier. His world was in order—just as he planned.

But in January 1955, winter, ice, a curve, and darkness combined to change his life dramatically. As he was driving home from his liquor store, he went into a skid on an S curve and his car hit a utility pole. Roy was pinned inside, and his spine was twisted beyond its suppleness. When they worked him out of the car, he could hardly breathe. The gravity of the situation quickly became apparent. He was paralyzed from the chest down. His playing days were over.

Campanella

Roy still had the use of his powerful shoulders and arms, but that was all the once indestructible catcher could command.

He went through an agonizing therapy and was confined to a motorized wheelchair.

But his mind was as clear as a bell in sub-zero weather, and that's because his heart and soul were clean and always working.

"I accepted my wheelchair. The Good Lord gave me my life and I found out how much life means to me. I must do all I can for my family and all I can do for humanity. I have my Bible to read, my family to love, and the world to help. I cannot do what I did before; that's gone, I accept it. I have my wheelchair, I accept it. My children are doing fine and my wife and I are happy for everything we have.

"We never know what is in store for us, but with God's help we can ride out every problem. That's why the Campanellas' home is filled with love and laughter."

In the mundane world of sport, with all the asinine platitudes that abound, with all the inequities of talent and drive, one time-honored expression covers the entire Roy Campanella story: "You can't keep a good man down."

Campanella was a spring training coach with the Dodgers for many years. His autobiography was later adapted into a movie.

He was elected to the Baseball Hall of Fame in 1969. He died on June 26, 1993 in Woodland Hills, California.

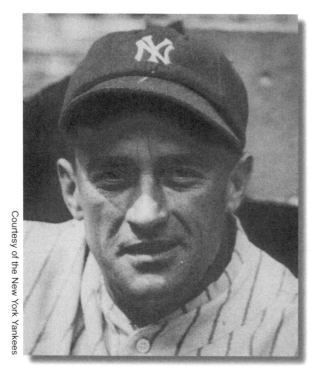

Courtesy of the New York Yankees

Tony Lazzeri was a member of the Yankees' greatest teams in the Ruth-Gehrig era. He was their dependable second baseman and a powerful hitter of frozen ropes to all fields, normally to right and right center, even though he was a right-handed batter.

Lefty Gomez, the Bombers' top left-hander, said Lazzeri was the smartest ballplayer he ever knew.

It should follow that he reaped the same reams of publicity and popularity that his fellow Yankees garnered for the domination of the American League—and the National League clubs they met in World Series play. But it doesn't.

Tony was a semi-recluse among the toasts of

Lazzeri

Broadway. He was not the subject of interviews, but rather, features were written about him.

He spoke in short sentences, mostly sport jargon, and seemed to have the worries of the Yankees on his own shoulders. He did not smile often. One writer said interviewing Lazzeri was like "mining coal with a nail file."

Tony was the unnamed captain of the infield with as objective a baseball mind as could be found.

In one game, Gomez had loaded the bases all by himself; the game was tight and Lefty seemed unglued. Lazzeri walked over to him and the crowd saw him say a few words to Gomez and then trot back to his spot at second base. Gomez got out of the jam with his hard strikeout pitches. But asked after the game what gems of wisdom Lazzeri had imparted to him, Lefty said, "He came over to the mound and said, 'You put those runners on there. Now you get out of this jam yourself.' So what could I do? He had me dead to rights!"

Lefty got back at him, though, in his own sweet Castilian way. One time with a man on first, the ball came back to Gomez on one bounce. He wheeled to second base where shortstop Frank Crosetti was cutting across the bag. So, without much ado, Gomez fired the ball to Lazzeri, ignoring the play at second. Asked why he

did it, Lefty said, "If Lazzeri is so damn smart, I just wanted to see what he'd do with the ball."

What was unknown to most people was the fact that Tony was subject to epileptic seizures. When scouted by the Yankees and their chief scout at the time, Bob Connery, the club received a note from Garry Herrman, Cincinnati Reds' president, who told the Yankee general manager, Ed Barrow, that the Reds had looked Lazzeri over but when they found out he was an epileptic they decided not to sign him.

Connery saw the power and fielding finesse of Lazzeri and wired Barrow: "I don't care if he has leprosy. Grab him." The rest is history.

For the record, he never had a seizure on the ball field and had only three while with the Yankees: once on a train and twice in hotel rooms. And these never presented a problem to anyone; club or personnel.

This quiet, solid workman and graceful exponent of the arts of second base had a quirk of nature that medicine had no cure for: he was a sneaky practical joker.

One time, Babe Ruth was dressing as fast as he could to make the bench in time for the National Anthem. He donned his socks and pants, but when he went to grab his shoes, he nearly pulled his arm out of its socket. The shoes would not budge. Tony had nailed both spikes to the floor of Babe's locker.

Many players would don their spikes and then feel pinched at the toes as they walked. Often they would tug their socks thinking they had bunched up. When that didn't work, they would sit on the bench and take their shoes off—and out would tumble just enough old cigarette butts to cause the discomfort.

Some players would arrive and find their sweatshirts tied into a single, large knot, which would be drenched with water to make it fuse like crazy glue. Sometimes when players put on their spikes, they would slide on like slippers—because Tony had removed their shoelaces. As a half-dozen irate players searched for a spare set of laces Lazzeri would be out on the field or sitting at his locker with a poker face and blank stare, seeing nothing and hearing nothing.

These shenanigans were Tony's contribution to the clubhouse atmosphere. His contribution with bat and glove was self-evident.

Lazzeri had come from humble immigrant parents in the San Francisco area. His dad, Agostino, a proud "new" American, had flags all over the house. He worked for the Union Iron Works as a molder. He exemplified the work ethic—work hard, be a good father, and pay the bills. He wanted Tony to follow him in the iron works. "Come to work and make a man of yourself with hard labor. It is good for you and you will make an honest living at it, too," he told Tony. The youngster worked in the mill for three years, all the while developing his strong hands and wrists. Almost six feet, he was slim of build, but the strength he gained in this hard labor served him well in baseball.

As a local star, he received nothing but opposition at home. Baseball, which his father said was "business for bums," came easy to Tony. And he gained regional fame with his powerful bat and swift fielding. He could play any position—and well. Primarily a shortstop, he joined the Pacific

Courtesy of the New York Yankees

Lazzeri takes a practice swing.

Lazzeri

Coast League and began a journey that led to the greatest team on earth. On the way, he did a number on the Pacific Coast League pitchers to the tune of 252 hits in 1925 along with 202 runs and 222 RBIs in 197 games; and averages of .354, .355 and .329. No wonder Bob Connery was strong in his recommendation.

Joining the Yanks as a shortstop in 1926, he got his feet wet in time for a .309 season in 1927, as the Yankees steamrolled the opposition from Game One through the World Series. In Series play, six with the New York and a cameo appearance with the Cubs in 1938, Lazzeri had twenty-eight hits including three doubles, one triple, four homers and nineteen RBIs.

His lifetime stats show solid across the board power

hitting: 6,297 at bats; 986 runs; 1,840 hits; 334 doubles; 115 triples; 178 homers; and 1,191 RBIs.

Although both his parents were Italian, Tony spoke little of their native tongue. In his faltering Italian, he was wont to jabber a few words across the infield to a fellow spaghetti bender, Frank Crosetti. It drove the base runners nuts, but Tony confessed, "Crosetti's Wop is awful."

He had a hearing loss, stemming from his years in the iron works. Thus, he was not eager to carry on conversations with any but his trusted teammates. When the Yanks dealt him to the Cubs in 1938, he was crushed. He always felt, as he said, "Once a Yankee, always a Yankee." He never made the big money of a Ruth or Gehrig but he made enough to invest. Some well meaning advisors counseled him to put his earnings into a well-known bank stock in his hometown, but the crash left him penniless. His Yankee salaries for his few remaining playing years were all he had left in earning power. But he took it as stoically as he did everything else. He shrugged, cried a bit, but then got down to work.

Lazzeri was a thoughtful man, seemingly attuned to the needs of others. Once, he called the room of a new reporter. In his usual gravelly, gruff voice, he said, "Could you come up to my room?" To the writer, who had only a nodding acquaintance with Tony, it seemed unusual. But when he knocked on Lazzeri's door, Tony glared at him and said sharply, "Why didn't you come into the clubhouse after the game?" It was an exhibition game in drink-dry Toronto (at that time). The writer said, "Why should I have? What was going on?"

"Didn't they tell you they had some real ale in there for us?" Tony asked.

"No," said the writer.

"Well, I figured you might like some," Lazzeri said. "So I brought you a couple of bottles."

"Tony," the writer said, "I wouldn't have been that thoughtful of you, or even another newspaperman."

"Look," said Lazzeri gruffly, "you're new and I just

didn't want to see you left out. That's all. Beat it. I'm going to bed. I'm tired."

At times he sounded mean, like when Boots Grantham tried to knock the ball out of Lazzeri's hand on a play at second. Tony got the ball to Gehrig, then whirled on Grantham. "If you ever try that again, I'll break your arm!"

Yet, when Miller Huggins, the Yankees' mite of a manager, died in September 1929, Lazzeri was one of the few Yankees who accompanied the body to Cincinnati, where the little guy was buried. Tony, who called Huggins "the greatest guy I ever met," was so crushed he went back to San Francisco and did not finish the season.

An important part of his baseball life was lost when Huggins succumbed to his fatal illness.

After his playing days, Tony retired to his beloved City by the Bay. He kept to himself for years, staying out of the way of reporters and even neighbors. After a number of years, perhaps after an inner struggle—or possibly he tired of the loneliness and yearned for the days when his fabled career had won him millions of adoring fans—Tony emerged from his cocoon. He started to go out and began to accept offers to speak at smokers and Communion Breakfasts. Quotes from Lazzeri began appearing in the *San Francisco Chronicle*, and a spark returned to his eyes. Life along the Barbary Coast was looking up.

But one day, in 1946, while he was alone, the Angel came.

His wife, Mary, returned from a short vacation and found him slumped at the base of a stairway, dead. He had been dead for a day and a half. Perhaps it was his heart, or maybe it was the fall.

The gruff voice was stilled, the great baseball brain faded away, an honest and skilled workman was assigned to the bench forever. A good man had died.

Lazzeri

Courtesy of the New York Yankees

Managers are supposed to force players to conform. They represent the establishment. And the establishment is exactly what Billy Martin challenged as a player.

An adequate player during his playing days with the New York Yankees and sundry other clubs from 1950 to 1961, Martin made more waves than base hits, and he made those waves all the way from Berkeley to the Copacabana.

Managing is understanding people. It's being able to convince players that they should be unselfish. While baseball people have long given Alfred Manuel Martin his due, they still argue about his character.

His manner, his style, his overall make-up—that special *it* that made Billy Martin tick—was like a

Martin

time bomb ready to explode. The trouble with Billy was that his reputation as being a detriment to the game always preceded him. As a result, most baseball purists would not admit that he excelled at managing a professional baseball team.

In fact, Martin did it better than any other man.

The record speaks for itself. The accomplishments he left in his wake border on the incredible. But his off-field antics are what many most remember him for.

There is no substitute for winning, and therein lay the basis of the Martin philosophy. Martin will not be remembered as the man who tied a Major League record in his first two at bats with a double and single. But he will probably never be forgotten for dismembering a toilet in the clubhouse after an especially excruciating loss to the Cleveland Indians.

Courtesy of the New York Yankees

Martin stretches for a line drive.

Billy Martin was emotional, intense, quick-tempered, and combative. But, on the other hand, he might very well have been the greatest teacher the game has ever seen. After all didn't he teach the Detroit Tigers how to bunt again?

Martin, described as a "small kid with a large nose," was born and raised in West Berkeley, California. He made himself into a baseball player

Martin

with an incredible amount of work. He also made himself the focal point of what seemed like every disagreement on the west coast.

He went on to become one of the most controversial players in a game filled with controversy. He later expanded his horizons to become the most memorable manager of the 1970s and 1980s.

He was the underlying reason for the success of the great Yankee teams of the 1950s. Teams loaded with personnel like Mantle, Berra, Rizzuto, and Ford. But, it was Billy Martin who served as the unofficial leader whether with his glove, his bat, or his fists. He was a regular for five years, and the Yankees finished in first place in each of those seasons.

And, while he went on to more-than-marginal success with every team he managed, Detroit, Texas, Minnesota, Oakland, it was still the New York Yankees that was his only true love. It has been said that every other team paid Billy Martin to manage except the Yankees.

As a fifteen and sixteen-year-old, he played pickup ball in the off-season in Berkeley with major leaguers. Martin signed with the New York Yankees in 1946 at the age of eighteen after a good, but for the most part unnoticed, high school career. It seemed that everyone thought he was too small, too weak, or too something.

"I was ecstatic," said Martin, "until I found out that Jackie Jensen was getting $60,000 to sign. I got zero."

Martin began in the minors with Idaho Falls in the Pioneer League. The next year he went to Phoenix in the Arkansas-Texas League, and toward the end of the season he was called up to Oakland, then in the Pacific Coast League. Martin batted an incredible .392 with 174 RBIs and forty-eight doubles at Phoenix before moving on. In Oakland, the manager was Casey Stengel, to whom Martin became "that little punk, how I love him." It was from Stengel that Martin learned the psychology of leadership.

In 1950 Martin moved east to Kansas City in the American Association after his first taste of spring training with the big leaguers.

He came to spring training as a brash kid and found himself in the locker room with the great New York Yankees. Joe DiMaggio was sitting there, and Stengel, his old manager, was stalking around the room mumbling something about a dropped fly ball three years earlier in a pick-up softball ball game.

It was the humbling experience that might just have made a player out of the kid, rather, the brat from Berkeley.

Ralph Buxton had played with Martin in 1949 at Oakland. Martin said that when he arrived at the Yankees training camp in 1950, Buxton had told the other players, "What a fresh little bastard, I was.

"Maybe I was a brat, but in my whole life I had never taken any crap from anybody, and I saw no reason why I should start then just because I was on the Yankees."

His locker was right next to DiMaggio. "Joe DiMaggio would come into the locker room and take his pants off and sit down in front of the locker. It struck me funny to sit there and watch a man take off his pants and sit there without taking his shirt off."

"We dressed side by side and one day I decided to do everything he did. He came in and took his pants off, I took off mine. And, then he asked for a half a cup of coffee and I asked for the same.

We'd both got the coffee and he spit into his spittoon (the only player I ever saw with a spittoon in his locker) and I tried to spit into his spittoon.

"Of course, I missed and he just stared at me. Then he mumbled: 'You fresh little bastard.' "

Martin didn't come up to stay until mid-season of that 1950 season when Stengel needed infield help. Martin remained in New York until 1957—with the exception of 1954—when he did his military service.

He established a Major League record for most hits in an inning in the first game in the Major Leagues (2) on April 18, 1950. Martin doubled and singled in the eighth inning in a comeback win over the Red Sox.

Playing with the Yankees in the 1952 World Series, he made the key play in the seventh game with a

Martin

Courtesy of the New York Yankees

Capturing the sequence of Martin's swing.

shoe-string catch of a bases-loaded pop fly by Jackie Robinson. The following year he had record-setting figures of 12 hits and a .500 batting average in the Series and was chosen its Most Valuable Player.

But there was that other side to Martin. He was a fighter. In 1952 and 1953, he was involved in brawls with the St. Louis Browns, and in 1957 he was the central figure in the "Battle of the Copacabana Night Club" that also starred Yogi Berra, Mickey Mantle, Johnny Kucks, Whitey Ford, and Hank Bauer. The incident eventually brought about his exile to the Kansas City A's.

On July 4, 1952, Martin was fined $100 and suspended for three days as the result of a fight in Yankee

Stadium. On December 17 of the same year, a $1,700 judgement was handed down against him in Oakland after an automobile accident.

In 1953, Hall of Fame second baseman Charlie Gehringer was quoted as saying, "Billy Martin is my kind of ballplayer."

A month after the 'Copacabana Incident' another fracas involving players from the Chicago White Sox proved to be the straw that broke the camel's back. On June 15, 1957, general manager George Weiss, who never seemed to warm up to

Courtesy of the New York Yankees

Martin throws to first in a double play combination.

Martin

the Martinese philosophy, traded him to the Kansas City Athletics in a four-for-three trade. Pitcher Ralph Terry and outfielders Woodie Held and Bob Martyn went to the A's along with Martin for pitcher Ryne Duren and outfielders Jim Pisoni and Harry Simpson.

Thus began the tumultuous and nomadic wanderings of the brat from Berkeley.

"After I was traded, I wasn't the same player," said Martin. "I tried and tried, but I couldn't get my heart into it. It felt like my heart was broken. It was all downhill."

Martin batted .251 with ten homers and thirty-nine RBIs that year, and he found himself traded again.

Martin played regularly with the Tigers in 1958 and batted .255 with seven homers and forty-two

RBIs. On November 30, he was on his way again, this time to the Cleveland Indians.

In 1959, as a part-time player, playing some second, short, and third with the Indians, Martin managed .260 with 9 homers and 24 RBIs in just 73 games. Martin was sent packing by season's end, along with Cal McLish and first baseman Gordie Coleman to obtain second baseman Johnny Temple from the Cincinnati Reds.

Billy did not stay with Cincinnati long. He was shipped to the Milwaukee Braves for cash. Six pinch-hitting spots ended his brief National League career. He was traded to Minnesota, where he ended his playing career in the spring of 1962, after Twins' owner Calvin Griffith suggested that his playing days were over.

Just before the 1962 season, Martin was offered a $100,000 contract by a team in Japan. He rejected the offer because he was more interested in prolonging his career in the United States, at whatever level, and rehabilitating his image.

He explained in a *Sports Illustrated* article (June 2, 1975), "When I was released, I was determined to come back. I thought, 'I've got to stay in this game.' I was going to eat humble pie, but I had to prove to people in baseball that I was a different person than who they thought I was. I'd let them see the real Billy Martin. But some of the stuff would follow me wherever I went . . . I'll never get completely away from it. But they've taken so many cheap shots at me and I've won so often, I don't care anymore."

Martin served the Twins as a special assignment scout from 1962 to 1964, and then coached at third base for Sam Mele into the 1968 season, when Griffith asked him to go to Denver to manage.

At Denver, Martin brought a last-place team back to a respectable fourth-place finish and then was asked to move in for Mele back in Minnesota in 1969.

In 1969 Martin brought the Twins to a first place finish in the American League's Western Division with a 97-65 record. Despite the Twins success that year, it was not a quiet year in the Twin Cities.

He was awarded a one-round, one-punch decision over pitcher Dave Boswell in a fracas outside a restaurant. In another incident he was arrested in a bar and subsequently given a three-day suspension by American League president Joe Cronin.

Martin was fired at the end of the season and spent 1970 learning the radio business with a friend.

He received calls from Charlie Finley about going to the A's. After talking with Finley, he decided against that marriage opting for the radio. It would prove to be the first year out of baseball for Martin since before high school.

In late 1970, he was hired as manager of the Detroit Tigers, and from 1971 to 1973, guided that club to second, first, and third-place finishes in the American League's Eastern Division. Again there was friction with the front office, and Martin was replaced by Joe Schultz on September 1, 1973. The official reason given for his dismissal was "failure to cooperate with executive policies."

One week later Bob Short, an old friend, brought him to Texas to turn the Rangers' fortunes around. He replaced interim manager Del Wilbur on September 8 to "evaluate talent for eventual off-season trades."

The 1973 Rangers lost over 100 games, yet Martin, ever bubbling with excitement and perhaps forgetting his humble pie, predicted that the Rangers would not only rise in the standings in 1974, but be a prime contender.

He was named the 1974 American League Manager of the Year after he guided the Rangers to a second-place finish and an incredible 84-76 record. As the 1975 season unfolded, Martin again experienced difficulties with the executive branch, and on July 21, when the Rangers stood in forth place, he was replaced by Frank Lucchesi.

On August 2, Martin replaced Bill Virdon as manager of the New York Yankees. The Yankees finished 30-26 under their new leader and finished third in the American League's Eastern Division.

The team would win the 1976 pennant and face the Cincinnati Reds in the World Series. His record was 97-62, yet his non-success in the Series (they lost in four straight) brought critics out in full bloom. But Steinbrenner had signed his field general to a three-year extension before the Series.

Sports Illustrated again described Martin as possessing "powerful qualities of organization, inspiration, evaluation, and attention to detail that makes him nearly peerless among managers. He makes all field decisions, juggling lineups, and habitually takes brave chances believing that the manager who runs scared usually gets beat."

As manager, Martin brought erring players into line with as little personal embarrassment to them as possible. "Stengel showed me how you don't even have to mention names to discipline," said Martin.

Despite the incredible wake of turmoil he seemed to constantly generate, Martin was reportedly well-liked by his players, partly because they knew that his notorious aggressiveness, intensity, and abrasiveness were on their side.

"There's no reason for me to get in a fight now . . . no man-to-man for me anymore," he said, "except to protect the players."

Off the field his democratic closeness to the players took such unorthodox forms as having a drink with them, a practice traditionally avoided by major league managers.

Martin followed with a 100-62 record in 1977 and led the Yankees to the World Championship and was en route to a repeat performance when he was discharged in a tearful adieu on July 24 of the following year. That was the first official canning—in reality a forced resignation for comments made about Reggie Jackson and the boss himself. The Yankees would go on to win the World Series under Bob Lemon.

In between though, in fact just five days after his discharge, he would run out on the field to a thunderous ovation from a packed stadium in an old-timer's game. It could only happen in New York.

Then it was June 19, 1979. This time it was Lemon

who got fired or was forced to resign and Martin who was hailed as the savior. But there would be no pennant in this, the stormiest year for the pinstripers since 1966 and Martin was canned again in October. He got the ax as the result of a go-round with a man named Joseph Cooper. And, what was Mr. Cooper's job? He was a Minnesota marshmallow salesman—it could happen only to Martin.

The years in Oakland followed as Martin "rebuilt" yet another distressed franchise into a contender. The lowly A's, since the bargain basement antics of Charlie Finley, were nothing but a Triple-A ball club in major league uniforms.

With the arrival of Martin came the "Dawn of Billy Ball."

It was in truth a "rebirth of baseball" in the Bay area. The 1980 A's finished 83-79 in second place. The following year, Martin was named *The Sporting News* Manager of the Year after leading the A's into the league playoffs. Oakland finished first with a 37-23 record during the first half of the strike-plagued season and 27-22 (second place) over the second half.

In 1982 the A's with a host of "tired arms" limped home at 68-94 in fifth place some twenty-five games behind division winner California. Ricky Henderson stole 130 bases, but more than 100 complete games over the last few years had probably ruined the

pitching staff. And, what a staff it could have been with Matty Keough, Mike Norris, Rick Landford, and Steve McCatty.

He was then out of work in Oakland, unceremoniously axed the night of the seventh game of the World Series. The options were threefold . . . go back to New York, manage in Cleveland, or go fishing and hunting for the next three years on the Oakland A's.

Before firing him, Oakland president Roy Eisenhardt had given the Cleveland Indians and New York Yankees permission to talk with Martin. Gabe Paul, the president of the Indians, reportedly made a three-year $1 million offer while Steinbrenner waited in the wings. But, on January 10, 1983, Martin replaced Clyde King as manager of the Yankees.

And, now he was back in New York, for what seemed like the umpteenth time. After a three-year hiatus, Martin was doing what he did best—managing the New York Yankees—the third time in eight years.

The fifth-place finish of the proud Bronx Bombers in 1982 had been a bit too much for George Steinbrenner. Billy would bring them back.

How long would the faithful have to wait for the deeply enriching spectacle of Billy Martin in pinstripes kicking dirt on yet another umpire?

Courtesy of the New York Yankees
Managing the Yankees.

The third inning, April 5, 1983 against Seattle, the familiar scene was that of Billy rushing on the field to engage the arbiter at second base and protest another call, stamping and gesticulating, the long vein on the left side of his neck showcased.

It just had to happen because it was part of the man. No one really knows whether or not he did it for show, for principle, or for the team. One thing is for sure, Steinbrenner wouldn't have it any other way.

The cover of the New York media brochure, which was sold commercially to unsuspecting fans, depicts the feisty one pointing a pedagogic finger in the face of a baseball arbiter. The television commercial pumping ticket sales shows an innocent dugout wall being accosted by Martin. It was all designed and

contrived to sell tickets. Steinbrenner was selling tickets and inviting the family out to a night of watching this man of baseball in his own captivating style.

Yes, Billy was back.

But, as quick as Billy was back, Billy was gone again.

Steinbrenner, who vowed when he hired Martin that this time would be different, fired him for a third time on December 16, 1983 and replaced him with Yogi Berra.

Martin, who had four years left on a five-year, $2 million contract, remained as a chief advisor to the owner. He acted as the chief aide in making trades and working with minor league personnel.

It marked the sixth time that he had been fired as a major league manager.

Billy Martin died in an auto accident on December 25, 1989.

Martin

Baseball Hall of Fame Library, Cooperstown, NY

H arry Caray with his tell-it-like-it-is style of broadcasting became as synonymous with Chicago baseball as the ivy that lines the center field wall in Wrigley Field.

Caray, who got his start in major league broadcasting in 1945, began broadcasting Chicago Cubs games on WGN-TV and WGN Radio in 1982. The year 1994 marked Caray's fiftieth anniversary as a sportscaster. In the spring of 1994, he was awarded the National Association of Broadcasters Hall of Fame Award.

This veteran play-by-play announcer was perhaps best recognized for his tradition of singing "Take Me Out to the Ball Game" during the seventh inning stretch and for his famous exclamations, "It might be, it could be, it is! A home run!" and "Holy Cow!"

Caray reached a major milestone on July 23, 1989, when he was honored as the winner of the Ford Frick Award at the annual induction ceremonies at the Baseball Hall of Fame in Cooperstown, New York. During his five-minute acceptance speech, Caray said, "The more I think of all the history which surrounds me, the more inadequate I feel."

In 1989, Caray was inducted into the American Sportscasters Association Hall of Fame located in New York.

It was in St. Louis, covering the Cardinals from 1945 to 1969, where Caray gained national fame. He was named Baseball Announcer of the Year for seven years in a row by *The Sporting News* for his work with the Cardinals.

After a quarter of a century in St. Louis, Caray moved to California to announce the Oakland A's games on television and radio during the 1970 season. The following year, Caray came to Chicago to become the radio/television voice of the cross-town Chicago White Sox, a position he held until 1981.

Caray was born Harry Christopher Carabina of French-Rumanian and Italian parentage in one of the poorest sections of St. Louis. He was an infant when his father died. At ten, he was taken in by his aunt upon the death of his mother.

As a young man, Caray played baseball at the semi-pro level for a short time before auditioning for a radio job at the age of nineteen. He then spent a few years learning the trade at radio stations in Joliet, Illinois, and Kalamazoo, Michigan. Caray did play-by-play for the St. Louis Hawks professional basketball team (now the Atlanta Hawks), the University of Missouri football team, and he announced three Cotton Bowl games.

After having never missed an opening-day pitch in forty-one years, Caray was absent from the booth for the preseason and more than a month of the regular season after suffering a stroke in February 1987. Caray overcame paralysis and speech difficulty to resume his play-by-play work in the Wrigley Field broadcast booth on May 19, 1987.

Caray's son, Skip, who once described his father as " . . . a mediocre singer but a hell of a broadcaster," has followed in the Caray broadcasting tradition. Skip Caray is the long-time voice of the Atlanta Braves and is a National Basketball Association announcer. In 1989, Skip's son Chip was hired as the play-by-play voice of the NBA's Orlando Magic, marking the first time three generations have broadcast major sports at the same time. In the spring of 1998, Chip Caray, succeeded his legendary grandfather as the voice of the Chicago Cubs on WGN.

Caray passed away on February 18, 1998; he was 83 years old.

Palermo

From the time he began his career as an American League umpire in 1977, Steve Palermo was widely regarded as one of the best umpires in the game. In fifteen years on the field, he brought boundless energy and enthusiasm to a game that he loved.

Steve was born on October 9, 1949, in Worcester, Massachusetts. He studied education at Norwich University, Leicester Junior College, and Worcester State College before attending the Umpire Development Program in 1972. His minor league career included work in the New York-Pennsylvania, Carolina, Eastern and American Association Leagues. He also worked winter baseball in the Florida Instructional, Dominican Republic, and Puerto Rican

Leagues. In 1977, after only five short years in the minor leagues, Steve joined the American League umpiring staff.

His career highlights include two of the most famous games in New York Yankees history. In 1978, he worked the Yankees one-game playoff against the Boston Red Sox in Fenway Park to determine the Eastern Divisional winner. In fact, it was Palermo, serving as the third-base umpire, who signaled "fair ball" when Bucky Dent hit the game-winning home run. On July 4, 1983, he worked behind the plate for Dave Righetti's no-hitter against the Red Sox at Yankees Stadium.

His career as an umpire also included the 1983 World Series, four American League Championship Series (1980, 1982, 1984, and 1989), and the 1986 All-Star Game. In August 1991, *The Sporting News* ranked Steve number one among American League umpires for overall performance.

In early July 1991, it seemed that Palermo's career might have ended, but everyone knows it is difficult to win an argument with an umpire, and Steve refused to lose this one.

On July 7, 1991, Steve and several friends were dining after a Texas Rangers game when they were alerted that two waitresses were being mugged in the parking lot. In an attempt to apprehend the assailants, Steve suffered a bullet wound to his spinal cord, resulting in instant paralysis to the lower extremities. Doctors told Steve and his wife, Debbie, that he would probably never walk again. Yet, through rehabilitation and a lot of determination, Palermo is winning his argument—he is walking with the use of one small leg brace and a cane.

On December 1, 1992, the Steve Palermo Foundation for Spinal Cord Injuries formally opened its doors. The foundation was formed to fund research for the discovery of a cure for paralysis while also providing hope and support to those with spinal cord injuries and their families—helping them get "One Step Closer to Home."

Since Steve's injury, he travels the country, relaying

his message of "Never Admit Defeat" to corporations and organizations nationwide. He is a highly regarded motivational speaker. In 1994, Steve was named special assistant to the Commissioner of Major League Baseball. From 1996 to 1997, he provided feature reports and served as a color analyst for Madison Square Garden Communications Network, the then cable network for the New York Yankees. In 2000, Steve was named supervisor of umpires, an additional role he now plays with Major League Baseball.

On January 1, 1995, the Steve Palermo Foundation

Courtesy of the Worcester Telegram & Gazette

Steve and his wife, Debbie, in 1992.

Palermo

for Spinal Cord Injuries merged with the Kent Waldrep National Paralysis Foundation becoming the Steve Palermo Chapter of the National Paralysis Foundation. Both families firmly believe that the consolidation of the two foundations would be a giant step in bringing the issue of paralysis to the national forefront. The same drive and dedication that returned Palermo to his feet will fuel the efforts of this chapter and foundation to aid in the discovery of a cure for paralysis.

Steve, his wife Debbie, and their boxer dog, Bently, currently reside in Overland Park, Kansas.

Rico Petrocelli joined the Boston Red Sox in 1965 as a shortstop, who would develop a powerful stroke at the plate. His bat guided him into the club's record books, but it was his family that guided him as a person.

For Petrocelli, his wife and children came first. So, at times, the everyday schedule of baseball was a tough thing to handle. He was not fond of the long road trips and the demands that travel put on his life. But his commitment to being a father and a husband did not prevent him from excelling at the game of baseball.

The young shortstop came of age in 1967 when the club reached "The Impossible Dream." He had climbed up through the minors and took over the

Petrocelli

regular shift at short after joining the Red Sox in 1965. It was in 1967 that he began to really shine.

"It was then that I realized that the main thing was to win the pennant," he said. "I don't think I really became a big leaguer until then."

In Game Six of the 1967 World Series, with the Sox down three games to two, Petro opened the scoring with a homer. He followed with another blast in the fourth to help force a seventh game.

Petrocelli exploded in 1969. He hit .297, posted a slugging percentage of .589, and set an American League record by hitting forty home runs as a shortstop (broken by Seattle's Alex Rodriguez with forty-two in 1998). He tied the record for fewest errors by a shortstop with fourteen.

Petrocelli rose to become the seventh player in Red Sox records for most home runs, RBIs, and extra-base hits thanks to continued success after moving to third base when Luis Aparicio joined the team at shortstop.

Rico Petrocelli excelled in a game that keeps its players on the road for much of the season, by balancing it with the family life that was so dear to his heart. That inner passion helped make Petro 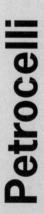 one of the greatest infielders ever to play for the Boston Red Sox.

After the 1976 season, Petrocelli retired after playing for thirteen seasons. He worked as a minor league coach for more than ten years, mostly in the Red Sox organization. From 1986 to 1997, he was a manager and hitting coach in the Chicago White Sox and Red Sox organizations.

Petrocelli was voted into the Boston Red Sox Hall of Fame in 1997. He has a career total of 210 home runs and 773 RBIs. He holds the Red Sox record for most consecutive games at third base without an error (77). His .589 slugging percentage in 1969 was the highest finish of any shortstop in baseball history.

Courtesy of the Worcester Telegram & Gazette

Rico warms up before a game.

He was picked for five All–Star teams and played in two, 1967 and 1969, and was known as one of the league's best fielders for over a decade.

He currently lives in southern New Hampshire with his wife, Elsie. He is the president of Petrocelli Sports Marketing and works at baseball clinics and in radio.

Petrocelli

Courtesy of the Los Angeles Dodgers

Lasorda

Regarded by many as baseball's most popular ambassador, Tommy Lasorda has served in the Dodger organization for more than half a century. He was named vice president on July 29, 1996, after retiring as manager, a position he held for the previous twenty seasons. Lasorda assumed all player personnel responsibilities when he was named the Dodgers' interim general manager on June 22, 1998. He relinquished his general manager duties when he was promoted to senior vice president on September 11, 1998.

In his current front-office capacity, Lasorda spends much of his time scouting, evaluating, and teaching minor league players as well as spreading baseball goodwill to thousands as he makes more than 100 speeches and appearances to various charities, private groups, and military personnel each year.

The 2000 season proved to be a memorable one for Lasorda. On May 5 of that year, he was named manager of the United States Olympic Baseball Team for the 2000 summer Olympic Games in Sydney, Australia. His team, considered underdogs by many, won the Gold Medal on September 27, five days after Lasorda celebrated his seventy-third birthday. On November 6, the Tom Lasorda Heart Institute at Centinela Hospital Medical Center in Inglewood, California officially opened.

In 1997, Lasorda was elected to the National Baseball Hall of Fame by the Veteran Committee in his first year of eligibility. He was the fourteenth manager and the fifteenth Dodger inducted into the Hall of Fame. Lasorda's uniform number 2 was retired by the Dodgers on August 15, 1997, and the main street that leads to the entrance of Dodger Town in Vero Beach, Florida was renamed Tommy Lasorda Lane. Lasorda also threw out the first pitch in Game Seven of the 1997 World Series.

Lasorda compiled a 1,599-1,439 record and won two World Championships, four National League pennants, and eight division titles in an extraordinary twenty-year career as the Dodgers' manager. He ranks thirteenth in wins and twelfth with 3,038 games managed in Major League history.

At the time of his retirement in 1996, Lasorda's sixteen wins in thirty National League Championship Series games managed were the most of any manager. Atlanta's Bobby Cox now holds the record with twenty-six wins in forty-nine games managed.

His sixty-one post season games managed rank third all-time behind Cox and Casey Stengel. Lasorda posted a 3-1 record as the N.L. manager in four All-Star games. He joined St. Louis' Gabby Street (1930–31) as the only managers in National League history to win league titles in his first two seasons when he led the Dodgers to titles in 1977 and 1978. Lasorda also managed five of the Dodgers'

Courtesy of the Los Angeles Dodgers

Tommy Lasorda makes a point.

Lasorda

sixteen Rookies of the Year, more than any other big league skipper in history.

Prior to replacing Hall of Famer Walter Alston as manager on September 26, 1976, Lasorda spent four seasons in Los Angeles on Alston's coaching staff from 1973 to 1976. He spent eight seasons as a manager in the Dodgers' minor league system at Pocatello (1965), Ogden (1966–68), Spokane (1969–71), and Albuquerque (1972). Lasorda also spent four years as a Dodgers scout after retiring as a player following the 1960 season. An astounding seventy-five players who Lasorda managed in the minor leagues went on to play in the majors.

Lasorda compiled a 0-4 record and 6.52 ERA as a left-handed pitcher in parts of three major league seasons with the Brooklyn Dodgers (1954–55) and Kansas City Athletics (1956). In all, he spent fourteen seasons in the minor leagues (1945–1960), and he served two years in the military from 1946 to 1947.

Lasorda has won numerous awards throughout his career, including: Minor League Manager of the Year by *The Sporting News* in 1970; Manager of the Year by United Press International and the Associated Press in 1977; Manager of the Year by the Associated Press in 1981; and National League Manager of the Year by Baseball America and Co-Manager of the Year by *The Sporting News* in 1988. He was the recipient of the Association of Professional Baseball Players of America's inaugural Milton Richman Memorial Award with Sparky Anderson in 1987, and has been recognized by many other groups. Lasorda has been a spokesperson for the American Heart Association and has received honorary doctorate degrees from Pepperdine University, St. Thomas University, California State University, Long Beach and the University of Phoenix.

Lasorda and his wife, Jo, have been married for over fifty years and reside in Fullerton, California. He was elected to the National Italian American Sports Hall of Fame in 1989.

BOXING

Boxing got its first glimpse of Italian Americans in 1895 when Casper Leone (Gaspar Leone) became the first Italian to win a championship title.

Leone was followed by Franke Conley (Francesco Conte) who won the Bantamweight Championship on February 22, 1910, when he knocked out Monte Atell forty seconds into the round.

A great number of Italian-American boxing champions would follow. Among them, Rocky Marciano, who won the World Heavyweight Championship when he stopped Jersey Joe Walcott in the thirteenth round in 1952. Marciano retired as undefeated World Heavyweight Champion on April 27, 1956. Marciano's record was 49-0 with forty-three knockouts.

Probably the greatest boxer ever was Willie Pep (Gugielmo Papaleo) who fought 242 bouts, winning 230. Pep began his career as an amateur boxer in 1938 and quit the ring twenty-eight years later in 1966. Pep was forty-three. He was the most brilliant featherweight champion in ring history.

Marciano was the first Italian inducted into the National Italian American Sports Hall of Fame in 1977. Pep was elected into the Hall of Fame the same year.

It was Fayetteville, North Carolina, in 1948 and Skeeter Scalzi was running the rookie camp for the Chicago Cubs. Scalzi was waiting for a rookie catcher to take his turn at bat. The kid looked promising. He was about five feet, eight inches tall, weighed about 185 pounds, and seemed to be all muscle.

When the rookie stepped up to the plate, he had Scalzi's complete attention—but not for long. The kid looked awful. Scalzi tried him behind the plate, but the kid couldn't throw out his mother, and when Scalzi told the kid to circle the bases, it took forever before the kid touched home.

"What's his name?" Scalzi asked.

"Rocco Francis Marchegiano," was the reply.

Marciano

"Hey kid," Skeeter told him, "you'd better go home before you get hurt."

Little did Scalzi know that this kid almost never got hurt, and instead of throwing his opponents out, he hit them with everything but the kitchen sink.

The kid's name was later changed to Rocky Marciano, and he became a world champion—but not on a ball club. He won fame in the ring instead of on the diamond, but he was 24-karat all the way, and baseball's loss was boxing's gain.

Meeting Scalzi years later, Rocky said, "I know I was a poor catcher, but I always thought I could hit."

Skeeter told him, "You sure proved you can hit, but not with a baseball bat!"

When Rocky was starting out, he fought as an amateur in club fights, the Golden Gloves, and in Army bouts as an enlisted man.

Along the way, there was one special fight in western Massachusetts. His longtime buddy Allie Colombo remembers it well.

"We were put up in a room above a garage in Holyoke. It was March 17, 1947, and Rocky was still in uniform and stationed at Westover Field in Springfield, Massachusetts. Since it was St.

Patrick's Day, we called him Rocky Mack.

"A fight was arranged with promoter Oriele Renault. When Renault came into the locker room and offered us thirty-five dollars, I told Rocky to put his clothes back on. 'You're crazy,' said Renault. 'I never pay more than that for a prelim.'

"Rocky looked at me like I was nuts, but he started to put his clothes on, and I told Renault that it was fifty dollars or no fight. The crowd in the arena did not like the long wait, so the promoter promised us fifty dollars and told us to get moving."

"Rocky won the fight and I was handed twenty dollars by an accountant. I yelled, 'Hey, you promised us fifty bucks!'

"The accountant said, 'No, it was thirty-five dol-

Marciano lands a strong right hand.

lars, and the boxing license cost fifteen dollars, and fifteen dollars from thirty-five is twenty dollars.'

"Rocky grabbed the man by the shirt. The accountant begged off, saying he'd talk to Renault.

"The creep came back," Colombo said, "with two policemen to toss us out, but Rocky pinned the cops to the wall.

"They asked if we had a written contract, and I said, 'No,' so the cops told us to take the twenty dollars and scram. I darted into Renault's office, and Rocky let go of the cops and came to the office door. 'Let me butt this guy just once,' he yelled.

"Without any more debate, Renault hands me thirty-five dollars and says, 'That's all. Now get outta here.'

"Rocky was still blazing mad, but I grabbed him by the arm and pulled him all the way out to the street. I showed him the thirty-five dollars plus the twenty dollars from the accountant, so we made five dollars extra. With that, Rocky hauled me into the nearest bar, saw a few guys in it and tells 'em all, 'The drinks are on me!' It cost us $4.50, so we made fifty cents extra. But it wasn't all profit. Rocky busted his left hand when he broke the guy's ribs."

When Rocky got out of the service, he went to work to help his family. He played football with the Brooklyn Pros—and he was a great linebacker. He also dug up roads for the gas company, helped build the Army's Camp Standish, and had a hundred other pickup jobs.

But boxing was always on his mind, and he wanted to gain experience as an amateur boxer. That one pro fight that Marciano had under an assumed name in Holyoke seemed to threaten his amateur standing. But he wisely took the advice of an amateur boxing official who told him to forget that he had ever had that fight.

Marciano then became the best amateur fighter in New England. But he lost in the Eastern Championships to Coley Wallace. That was the first and last time he ever lost a fight. And after that bout, he turned pro.

Marciano

Allie Colombo knew Rocky needed grooming, and he sought out trainer Charley Goldman for help. Colombo took Marciano to Goldman's gym, and if it wasn't for Rocky's powerful right hand, Goldman would never have paid attention to him.

"Rocky was awful, really. He would shoot a jab with his palm up. In his normal stance, his feet were thirty-seven inches apart. He fought straight up, and he dropped his right foot back when he threw a punch with his right, so he was never in position to follow up with another punch. I put him in against one of our club boys, and my boy made Rocky look like a kid with jabs, hooks, and overhands. Rocky took everything my boy threw at him, and then his right hand came around like a pile driver and hit my boy in the stomach. I had to call time and get him breathing again. No one can teach a punch like Rocky had, so I kept him," Charley said.

Colombo knew Rocky would need a good manager to get fights, so he checked with Goldman, read the papers, and made a few calls. It was agreed that Al Weill was the best man for the job. Weill checked out Rocky and then conferred with Goldman, who was honing the block of granite into a

Rocky Marciano with his championship belt.

boxer's form. Afterward, Weill decided to be Rocky's manager.

"There were many times I wanted to chuck the whole thing," Goldman said, "but Rocky asked for work, and he never forgot or undid what he was taught. He always improved. Al got him a few fights that couldn't go elsewhere. None were setups, but they were guys who wouldn't draw in New York, so he'd book 'em against Rocky near his hometown, where Rocky was the draw against anybody."

Weill maneuvered Rocky like a chess piece. Rocky had beaten Roland LaStarza in a gruelling match, and then he dropped Joe Louis into a crumpled mass at the ropes and ended Joe's hopes of ever coming back. Finally, Weill got Rocky a fight with

the reigning world champion, Jersey Joe Walcott in Philadelphia on September 23, 1952.

Both fighters were tuned to perfection for the fifteen-round bout. Walcott was a cagey slugger whose age was beginning to show. Marciano was a bullish slugger with youth on his side. But Marciano had something else going for him. He had dogged determination, a drive to win no matter how many punches he took.

In the first round, Walcott dropped Rocky for an abbreviated count of four. "I got up quickly because I wasn't hurt. I was just so mad at myself," Rocky said afterward.

Round after round, the two men put on a slugfest. Each man was bloodied and each had blood on their gloves. By the thirteenth round, it seemed impossible that the fight would go the distance. And it didn't. Rocky came out fast and piled a right hand into Walcott's jaw that drove the consciousness from his body. Walcott sagged and collapsed. He could hear the referee counting, but he could not respond.

At the count of "Ten" Rocky leaped in the air with his hands raised and let out a yell. Colombo ran into his arms. They clung together in silence.

CHAMPION OF THE WORLD. It did not sink in until later when Rocky had his wife, Barbara, in his arms. It was when she said, "Champ" that he realized what he had accomplished.

A classic Marciano fight was the unforgettable Archie Moore bout on September 21, 1955 at Yankee Stadium. Moore was an old, crafty, great counter puncher with the experience of twenty years barnstorming for 300-dollar purses in tank towns. But Rocky had a stomach made of steel. He could take whatever was thrown at his midsection without a grimace. It simply made no impression on him. He just kept coming, throwing punch after punch, and each punch was a stinger.

Rocky came into the ring wearing a blue robe with white trim. Archie had a creation of black brocade trimmed in gold, with Louis XIV cuffs and brilliant gold lining. Archie had a vocabulary that would astound his listener and a braggadocio that befit a politician. Rocky had simple words of apology, "You know how awkward I am and how clumsy, too."

The first round was a sparring match. Archie danced and picked his shots, catching Rocky again and again. But Archie's blows fell on Rocky's shoulders and arms. In the second round, Marciano led with his right. Moore countered quickly, and Rocky went down. His left eye was bleeding, but as usual Marciano hopped up early. He was cut, but otherwise unhurt, and he was mad at himself for getting decked.

Archie's experience told him that time had come for the kill. But Archie's experience did not include fighting Marciano. Rocky came at Moore with a barrage of punches. Moore fought back with everything he had, landing punches from Marciano's head to his belly button. Though he jarred Rocky a few times, Archie could not stop his opponent. All he could see was the killer eyes boring into him.

Just before the bell, Rocky nailed Archie with a right hand that brought stars to Moore's eyes. Archie said later that between rounds he asked himself, "What in hell did I do wrong?" The answer was "Nothing." Moore did all he could do; Marciano simply was something Archie had never before encountered.

Rocky put on his planned attack that was the equivalent of saturation bombing. He buried Archie with punishing blows one after another. At the end of the sixth round, Moore was a battered hulk. The doctor wanted to end it, but Moore looked him in the eye and said, "No, if I lose, I have to go out like a champion."

He carried the fight to Marciano with jabs and flurries but took more punishment in the bargain. In the eighth, Archie went down again. He fought back in the ninth, but Rocky poured it on, clubbing him with both hands one punch after the other until Moore slumped to the canvas in his corner, exactly where his stool would have been. Like Walcott, he could hear the

referee counting, but he could not respond—his body was numb all over.

The fans never used the seats they paid for. Once this titanic fight started, they stood and cheered for all nine rounds.

After the fight, Moore drove the cobwebs from his mind and airily told the newsmen, "I think Rocky enjoyed it, and I hope the public enjoyed it, too."

Rocky ran his string of victories to forty-nine, and then he retired, an undefeated champion.

He was a formidable foe—relentless, undaunted, and unstoppable—the strongest fighter ever. And he was a man of great pride and consummate honesty.

Rocky took his retirement as seriously as he did his fighting. He devoted himself to his wife and kids, his relatives, his old friends and his new friends. He kept in shape, despite a tendency to put a few pounds on around his middle. He refereed a few fights and a few wrestling matches, had a couple of "computer fights" with Jack Dempsey and Mohammed Ali and made some personal appearances.

He kept a neat home with the metal cutout of himself in a boxing pose over his mailbox. The people of Brockton, Massachusetts, who knew Rocky before he became famous, treated him with a loving respect for what he did for the town.

Rocky hated to drive a car, and in his lifetime he never totaled more than 500 miles driving. Snarled traffic drove him crazy, and he became a bundle of nerves behind the wheel. Someone always drove him, even to his mother's house. He liked to sit up front and wave to people who recognized him and greeted him with waves or called out as he passed by.

Retirement was a life Rocky loved. He loved the people he spent it with and he loved the community he spent it in. Few could understand how a man who attained the heavyweight boxing championship of the world, and who was undefeated to boot, could turn his back on fame and hang out in his home town. Many in the sports world felt that he had forsaken them. That was because they never really knew Rocky. He was a talented young man who was handy with his hands, and an eager and willing helper, one who loved to "just be with his wife" and his relatives. He was a man who never forgot where he came from.

Rocky remembered that he had worked hard early on to develop his body. That process was aided by his mother's wonderful cooking. He also remembered that when he and Allie were first in the game and fighting for Al Weill, in order to stretch their dollars they ate in lots of greasy spoons and Mexican restaurants. Allie said the food was so bad, that if you belched you'd wonder why you ate it in the first place. It was only when Weill started booking Rocky in New York, that they began to eat in the best restaurants. After all, no fighter could "last" on junk food.

Rocky knew the glitter of the boxing world and he loved it. But he also knew that it was in his own world—his wife, family, and friends—that he found the real values in life. That is how he managed his retirement so easily. He returned to the real values, which he had really never left.

Tragedy was the only thing which could separate Marciano from his loved ones. A plane crash in Iowa on August 31, 1969, snuffed out the life of this indestructible human. He had been picked up by his friend, Frank Farrell, at a Chicago airport in a light aircraft and they headed for Des Moines, Iowa, where he was to appear at a testimonial dinner. Mechanical trouble caused the plane to crash in a desolate area near Newton, Iowa.

The wires poured out the news, the obituaries, the follow ups, pictures, and interviews. Rocky was in the headlines once more—but it was for the last time.

Throw away all the fight victories, all the championships, all the money, and all the glitter. What really happened when that plane crashed was that the world lost one hell of a human being.

Marciano

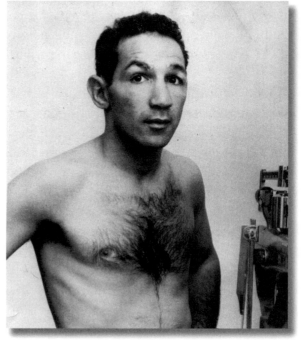

Pep

It was 1940—it was the kid's first four-rounder, and glancing across the ring at his opponent, he felt nervous. It was going to be a hard fight, he thought. The guy staring at him from the opposite corner looked like a bulldog. He had the mashed-in nose, the cauliflower ears, the puffy scar tissue over his eyes. A tough, ring-wise veteran, the kid thought. This guy's a real pro. I'm really gonna have to move. I'll have to go all out to win this one.

The kid rushed out at the bell and launched a whirlwind attack. Jabs that whistled like ricocheting bullets tattooed the bulldog's mangled nose as the kid ducked in and out, back and forth, beating a steady rhythm on the battered features of the old journeyman war horse.

Finally the bulldog grappled him into a clinch. "Hey, kid," he said. "What the hell are you doing? Lay off will ya? What're ya fightin' for, the championship of the world? Scatter your punches!"

Relaxing in the lobby of the Holiday Inn in Worcester, Massachusetts, Willie Pep chuckled when he recalled that early fight. "What did I know?" he said with a grin. "I was still just a green kid. I didn't know the tougher and more beat-up they looked the worse they were as fighters. I kept hitting the guy on the nose."

It's a long bumpy road that leads from the smoky club fight arenas of Holyoke, New Haven, and Hartford to the bright lights and glory of Madison Square Garden. An almost impossible journey it would seem for a skinny kid named William Papaleo of Hartford, a kid who looked too frail to be a fighter and who had trouble holding his own against the boys at the playground and school.

"It was a tough neighborhood and I was always getting into scraps," Willie recalled. "I never did too good. I always got beat up."

It was after one of those street brawls that a boy a couple of years older than Willie advised him that he should become a boxer. "You're always fighting anyway," he said. "Why not go down to the gym and get paid for it."

That sounded great to Willie. He hustled down to the Charter Oak Gym in Hartford, but the trainers laughed at him. He was too small. He was just a young green kid. The fighters would murder Willie.

"They chased me away," Willie recalled, "but I kept at it. A year later [1938], I was amateur [flyweight] champ at seventeen."

After winning the Connecticut State Amateur Bantamweight Championship in 1939, Willie turned professional. He then rewrote the record books and achieved fame as one of the greatest and most popular boxing champions of all time. Many claim he was unparalleled in the boxing skills, ring savvy, and popularity he brought to the featherweight division. In a storybook career that spanned an amazing twenty-six years and led Willie to the distinction of being the only fighter to be elected to the Boxing Hall of Fame while still actively pursuing his boxing career, he overcame long odds and fought back against tremendous adversity to endure and dominate in a sport that demands oceans of stamina, courage, and dedication. Willie Pep won more fights than any other boxer in the history of the sport compiling a record of 230 profession-al victories.

Willie Pep in a classic pose.

Pep

Pep came up in the days of Frank Sinatra, big bands, bobbysoxers and the ominous threat of World War II. He was a hungry kid with his sights on the moon. He fought two or three times every month for purses (fifty dollars was decent money for a guy on an undercard in those days) that would make the modern millionaire boxers laugh. He was fast and quick and he had a great deal of natural ability that he spent every available hour sharpening in the gym. But he was still a long way from the delicately defined rhythm and poise that would one day inspire comparison of Willie's performances with those of the greatest of matadors and artists.

He was coming up in that golden era of boxing

when there were many outstanding boxers but not enough big money fights to go around, the years before the financial bonanza of television and closed-circuit theater. There were no shortcuts to fame and fortune. It was a time when even great fighters had to pay their dues, scuffling and fighting wherever and whenever possible, waiting for their shots at the main events. It was a time when good fighters were plentiful and without the proper management would wind up broken down and used as cannon fodder for the young hopefuls who were always in the shadows, anxious to replace them.

But it all looked good to so many of them who had grown up hungry in the Great Depression of the 1930s. Fighting was a way to escape the drudgery of the factories and low-paying laborers' jobs. It was a ticket to the big time. And, if you were good enough and got the right breaks, the big money. Bright lights and flashy cars—wine, women and song. The Championship of the World! Those were the dreams and fantasies that kept the fight train express rolling.

And so Willie Pep came running. A kid so talented that in today's slickly marketed world of high-finance pugilistic spectaculars he would have been nurtured and pampered, spoon-fed and groomed from the very beginning, guided on a course that would lead quickly to the multi-million-dollar purses of television and closed-circuit programs.

In 1940, he had to pay his dues, pack a bag and travel light and rattle down the highway in an old jalopy. He boarded the Hartford express with whistle stops in Hartford, West Haven, Holyoke, New Haven, Manchester, New Britain, and Fall River. And he told himself, "Be careful, don't get cut. You gotta win tonight, but you gotta fight next week." It was a long and dangerous road from Hartford to Madison Square Garden. There was no way to make it without plenty of guts and a lot of luck.

And there was no way to make it without the proper guidance. Willie didn't like his manager in

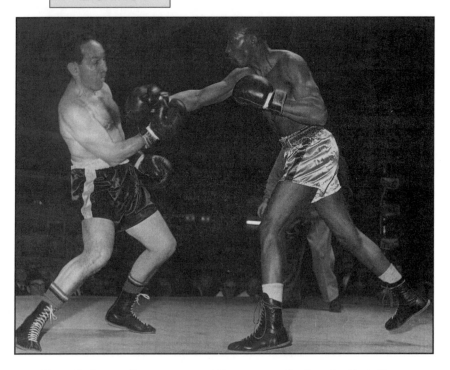

Pep fighting his most stubborn rival, Sandy Saddler.

Hartford, so, at eighteen, he left home and headed for the West Coast. A kid alone in unfamiliar territory, without a job or a manager, determined to make his living off the talent in his fists. But first he had to get some fights. He had to make enough money to eat.

A California gym owner offered Pep a dollar a round to spar with one of his fighters. Willie smiled when he recalled it. "I was boxing the greatest Mexican champ that ever fought, Manuel Ortiz. And here they were paying me a buck a round," he said.

It wasn't that bad, though, because Ortiz couldn't hit him. Will O' The Wisp was the nickname that would stick with Willie throughout his career. In and out. Fast as lightning with the moves and combinations. The opponent couldn't hit what he couldn't see. Willie's speed and agility would become his trademark. And the only times he abandoned his

Pep

trademark skills (against his most stubborn rival, Sandy Saddler) and tried to be a brawler, the results were disastrous.

The four bitterly fought, grueling, mauling grudge battles with Saddler were among Pep's toughest. Willie lost three of they fights—they were stopped by the referee because he was cut and badly hurt.

"I was winning the fights and they stopped them," Willie recalled. "Saddler was a tough, hard puncher. He KO'd more fighters than any featherweight in the world. But it was my own fault. I shouldn't have brawled with him. I was a strong guy but not like Rocky Marciano or Graziano. They were bulls. But I couldn't take that kind of punishment. If I got hit hard I got hurt. Saddler hurt me three times. You can't beat a guy at his own game. I'm a boxer. Hit and run. But I fought Saddler's fight. I wanted to be a tough guy, so I fought him."

The fights have been described as some of the dirtiest and roughest of all time. There was one widely distributed photograph that showed Pep, Saddler and the referee all sprawled on the canvas after the referee had failed in an attempt to break up the fighters' wrestling match. Willie said people got the wrong impressions. "I never went after guys like that, only Saddler," he said. "If I was hurting I never tried to use a cut or something for an advantage. If I cut a guy's eye, I wouldn't hit him there anymore. I was a boxer. I could beat the guy anyhow. You gotta have some feelings in there."

Pep gave up the ring for good after losing a decision to Calvin Woodland in 1966. "He was a real good prospect," Willie recalled, "a hell of a fighter. But I figured it was time to quit. Nobody can fight forever."

"I haven't got any of my fight money left," Willie said. "I was gullible. I was married five times and whenever I got divorced I left them with everything. I took care of them all. That's where my money went."

"I made more than a million dollars in the ring," he said, "but the guys today make more than that in one fight."

"What would you have done if you hadn't been a boxer, Willie?" a friend asked.

"I don't know," Willie answered. "I love horses. I love the track. I think I might have been a jockey."

After his retirement, Pep refereed fights and worked in a variety of public relations jobs throughout the country. He often made appearances that included lectures and showings of his fight films.

"I can't get the film of the fight that I beat Saddler," he said with a grin. "I can get the ones I lost but not that one."

Willie shrugs, and his grin broadens.

"That's life," he says.

Pep

—The section on Willie Pep was written by Everett M. Skehan author of Rocky Marciano: Biography of a First Son, *originally published by Houghton Mifflin. The paperback edition was published by Robson Book Ltd. It is used with Mr. Skehan's permission.*

Courtesy of Joe DeNucci

T he final days of the old Boston Garden were
a time of nostalgia. As the date drew closer
for its demolition to make room for the
new Fleet Center, the public address announcer
would recall the great events of the past, the athletes,
teams, and individuals that shook the rafters of the
venerable building.

Names like Cousy, Russell, Bird, Orr, Esposito,
Collins, DeMarco and Priest brought back vivid
images of many great moments in sports history.
Those memories have left an indelible mark that will
live for as long as sports are played in Boston.

When it came to boxing, there was one name that
stood alone in the spotlight, and that name was Joe
DeNucci. DeNucci fought, won more and scored

DeNucci

Courtesy of Joe DeNucci

Joe DeNucci attacks an opponent.

more knockouts than any other boxer in Garden history.

The late promoter Sam Silverman, who probably promoted more fights than any other promoter, once said of Joe DeNucci: "He was iron-chinned, courageous and a ferocious puncher."

Silverman went on to say that he believed that two of the greatest fights, if not the greatest in Boston, were the two that featured DeNucci against the legendary Emile Griffith. The bouts took place, back-to-back on September 16 and October 11, 1972. Both went the distance, with Griffith hanging on to win both by a narrow margin.

"Griffith retained his title, but it was DeNucci who gained the everlasting respect of the big crowd on hand. He proved he belonged with the best," said Silverman.

When DeNucci traveled to Lyon, France, in 1973 to fight European champ Claude Boutier, he was accompanied by Silverman. Silverman loved boxing, and in fact, he was coming home from a boxing event when he died in an auto accident.

Joe DeNucci, son of a YMCA maintenance man, rose from Golden Glove champion to the fifth ranked middle-weight in the world, at a time when the middle-weight division

Courtesy of Joe DeNucci

Joe DeNucci, Massachusetts State Auditor.

was the toughest division in boxing.

In 1956, while a sixteen-year-old student at Newton High School, in Massachusetts, DeNucci won the New England Golden Glove Championship. The following year, again while he was still a student in high school, DeNucci joined the professional ranks of boxing.

DeNucci fought, defeated, and hung in with the greatest names in the middleweight division, and one thing is for sure, Joe did not get rich. The most money he received for a fight—and a television fight at that—was $4,000. Today, TV six-rounders are picking up more than that.

When Joe was inducted into the Boston Chapter of the National Italian American Sports Hall of Fame, he was cited for his performance in and out of the ring.

DeNucci

DeNucci was a well-respected middleweight boxing contender. His talent shone brightly even as a sixteen-year-old when he won the Golden Glove Championship.

Always giving a commendable performance, DeNucci went on to a distinguished sixteen-year career, registering an impressive 65 wins, 12 losses, and 5 draws. More than thirty of his wins were by knockouts. As New England middleweight champ, he fought some of the finest middleweights in the world, including Griffith and Joey Giardello.

One hundred percent sums up the character of Joe DeNucci, known to many of his associates as the "Champ." For more than two decades, Joe has made an all out commitment to public service, first as a Massachusetts State Representative and for many years as the highly respected State Auditor—one of six constitutional officers elected statewide in the Commonwealth of Massachusetts.

Throughout his life, Joe DeNucci has earned a reputation for integrity, independence, and compassion.

The *Boston Herald* columnist, Joe Fitzgerald, who covered sports for twenty-five years, likes to tell the story of DeNucci's attendance at a Golden Gloves boxing event in Lowell, Massachusetts years ago. DeNucci was the center of attention, and another boxer reached through the crowd.

"Joe, I'm a nobody, but I just wanted to shake your hand," the man said. DeNucci stopped in his tracks. "If you ever climbed those three steps and stepped into the ring half-naked in front of all those people, don't you ever call yourself a nobody," DeNucci said. "I have the greatest respect for you."

"That's Joe DeNucci," Fitzgerald said. "Joe never forgot where he came from."

Courtesy of Tony DeMarco

DeMarco

I n the early and mid-1950s, a good-looking young Italian fighter from Boston became the most feared puncher in the welterweight division. He blasted his way to the top of the division, finally achieving a childhood dream of winning the Championship of the World.

His name was Leonard Liotta, but you would remember him better as Tony DeMarco. He was born on January 14, 1932. His father was a Boston shoemaker. When he began boxing as a youngster, Tony was a southpaw. His manager had a unique method for converting him to a right-hander: He would tie Tony's right hand to his chest, forcing DeMarco to learn to lead with his left during shadow-boxing and heavy bag exercises.

At age fifteen, he became a top amateur, losing only two fights, and finally reaching the point where very few amateurs were willing to get into the ring with him. To end this forced idleness, Tony decided to turn pro. He lied about his age, so he could get a license, and began punching for pay at sixteen. His first fight was on October 21, 1948, and he stopped a boy by the name of Hector Jones in the first round. Three weeks later he beat Jones again in two rounds. A knockout of Billy Shea and a win over George Silva made him 4-0 in his debutante year.

DeMarco fought seven times in 1949, losing a decision to Edward White, but winning six times, as he brought his knockout mark to eight in eleven fights. On January 9, 1950, Tony was stopped by Art Suffolatta in the fifth round when his manager called a halt to the bout. But Tony won his remaining seven contests that year. In 1951, DeMarco boxed eight times, winning four by knockouts, three on points, and being stopped in four rounds by Chick Boucher.

A big break came in 1952. He won his first four bouts, then got a call to substitute for Tony Pellone in a bout against Jackie O'Brien in Brooklyn, New York. It was DeMarco's first fight as a welterweight, and the 20-year-old Boston boy took the decision

from O'Brien. But things lagged after that, and he lost back-to-back decisions to Bryan Kelly and Gene Poirier.

In 1953, Tony went like wildfire. He fought eight times, winning his first six bouts by knockouts. The KO string included a five-round stoppage of top-rated Terry Young. On October 10, he won a ten-round decision from another DeMarco, future lightweight champion Paddy DeMarco. He went undefeated in seven fights during 1954, and by the end of that year Tony had scored 28 knockouts in his career of 50 bouts.

On February 11, 1955, DeMarco was matched with the world lightweight champion, Jimmy Carter. Tony was not in top form that night, and put up a bad fight. It was called a draw. But that bad fight was probably the luckiest break Tony ever got. Welterweight champ Johnny Saxton's managers were looking for an easy title defense for Saxton, prior to a big money match. They thought DeMarco would be safe, and figured they could draw a good gate in his hometown of Boston, so they matched Saxton with DeMarco, with the title on the line. They didn't plan on the outcome. DeMarco tore Saxton apart, dropped him, and in the fourteenth round, Tony pinned Saxton in a corner and unleashed one of the more savage beatings ever dished out in the welterweight division. Left and right hand bombs landed with deadly accuracy, and Saxton was completely defenseless and unconscious on his feet. Finally, and luckily not too late, the referee jumped in between them to protect Saxton, and signaled that Tony DeMarco was the new welterweight titleholder, as the delirious fans at Boston Garden shouted themselves hoarse.

But Tony's reign was to be brief. He knocked Saxton out for the crown on April 1, 1955. A little more than two months later, on June 10, DeMarco put the title on the line against Carmen Basilio. In a tremendous slugfest, Basilio outlasted the Boston Bomber, and took the welterweight throne out from under Tony's exhausted body, with a twelfth-round knockout.

However, the glory of Tony DeMarco was not yet over. Three months later, he knocked out Checo Vejar in one round and was signed for a rematch with Basilio. They met for the second time on November 30, 1955, and this epic battle was even more ferocious than their first meeting. The bruising, bloody battle was tabbed the "Fight of the Year." Many called it the fight of the decade, and few even went so far as to say it was the best welterweight contest of the modern era. The outcome was virtually a repeat performance, with Basilio outlasting DeMarco, stopping Tony again in the twelfth round.

In his next outing, on March 5, 1956, Tony knocked out the then lightweight king Wallace Bud Smith in nine rounds. On October 13, Tony defeat-

DeMarco

DeMarco, left, fights Carmen Basilio on June 10, 1955. Basilio won with a twelfth-round knockout.

DeMarco

ed former welterweight champion Kid Gavilan on points. He then dropped two decisions to Gaspar Ortega, ending the year. His first fight of 1957 saw him pitted against Ortega once again, and this time, Tony came out the winner. But on October 29, 1957, he was stopped in the fourteenth round of a non-title contest with future welterweight king Virgil Akins. In his only fight of 1958, he was knocked out again by Akins, this time after twelve rounds. Tony won twice in 1959 against minor opposition, then clashed with Denny Moyer on February 10, 1960. "I fought Moyer, but to this day I couldn't tell you what kind of fighter he was," recalls Tony. "It didn't last long enough, and there really wasn't much fighting. We banged heads, blood started flowing from me when the fight was just a few moments old, and it was stopped in the second round, Moyer a TKO winner without landing a good punch."

Tony had one outing in 1961, stopping former welterweight champ Don Jordan in two rounds. On February 6, 1962, Tony closed out his career with a decision over Stefan Redl.

He fought 71 times, with 33 knockouts among his 58 victories. He boxed one draw, with Jimmy Carter, and lost 12 times, 5 by decisions and 7 by knockouts. He recalls his fight with Saxton and his second bout with Basilio as being his greatest. "I felt I was ahead of Basilio both times, but Carmen had one thing I didn't—stamina. He knew he could go fifteen rounds, I, on the other hand, was great for ten rounds, but after that, it was anybody's guess," he said.

Following his retirement from boxing, Tony gave up his interest in a Boston restaurant and became a liquor salesman. He continued this line of work in San Francisco, then relocated to Phoenix, where he became a bartender. He now lives in Boston and is a regular at most professional fights in the Boston area.

Tony was elected to the National Italian American Sports Hall of Fame in 1981.

LaMotta

J ake LaMotta, perennial opponent of Sugar Ray Robinson, was a tough, smart fighter. He fought with a brutal will to win and was a master at playing possum in the ring. LaMotta's fame was given an extra dimension by the Academy Award-winning movie, *Raging Bull*, in which Robert DeNiro portrayed the fighter.

Born in New York, LaMotta was a street fighter who ran afoul of the law as a youth and spent some time in reform school. He began boxing in his teens, fought as an amateur for two years, then turned pro at the age of eighteen. He quickly made a name for himself, and by 1942 he was ranked by *The Ring* as the sixth-best middleweight contender. That year he fought Sugar Ray Robinson in the first of their six match–ups. LaMotta lost the ten-round decision, but in 1943, he became the first to beat the then undefeated Robinson. LaMotta also battled Hall of Famer Fritzie Zivic four times in seven months in 1943 and 1944, losing only once.

LaMotta lost two decisions to Robinson in 1945. He continued to box well, but was not given a chance at the middleweight title. Later, LaMotta testified before a U.S. Senate Anti-Monopoly Subcommittee that he was denied a title fight because he refused to become involved with mobsters. At the same hearings, however, LaMotta said he took a dive in a 1947 fight with Billy Fox in return for a promise that he could fight for the title.

On June 16, 1949, LaMotta finally got his chance at the middleweight title against Marcel Cerdan. The match was held at Briggs Stadium in Detroit before 22,183 fans. After he wrestled Cerdan to the canvas in the first round, injuring Cerdan's left shoulder, LaMotta easily controlled the fight. He knocked out Cerdan in the tenth round to win the World Middleweight Championship. There was never a rematch. On his way to the United States to fight LaMotta for a second time, Cerdan died in a plane crash in the Azores on October 27, 1949.

LaMotta had two amazing fights left in his career. In 1950, he scored a fifteenth-round knock-out over Laurent Dauthville. Dauthville, who dominated through most of the bout, fell victim in the twelfth round to LaMotta's trick of feigning serious injury. When Dauthville came in close, LaMotta unleashed a flurry of blows. LaMotta, still behind in the fifteenth, gathered the strength for one last foray. He knocked out Dauthville with thirteen seconds to go in the fight.

LaMotta lost his final fight with Robinson on Valentine's Day, 1951 in Chicago Stadium. The two seemed fairly well matched in the early going, but as time went on, Robinson's pummeling of LaMotta became painful to watch. That LaMotta

could still stand amazed the ringside experts. With LaMotta still on his feet but Robinson clearly the winner, the fight was stopped in the thirteenth round. LaMotta fought for another three years before turning to acting and other pursuits.

LaMotta was inducted into the International Boxing Hall of Fame in 1990. He was elected to the National Italian American Sports Hall of Fame in 1977.

From the farm country around Canastoga, New York sprang one of boxing's toughest heroes, Carmen Basilio. Twice welterweight champ, Basilio had the nerve to challenge—and beat—middleweight king Sugar Ray Robinson in one of the most brutal matches of ring history. An all-out fighter who took as may punches as he delivered, Basilio bore the badges of his profession on his angular face—flattened nose, scarred cheeks, and split eyebrow. Built low to the ground, Basilio was a game fighter who looked mean and who fought with great courage.

Basilio's father, Joseph, an onion farmer, was a boxing fan who inspired his son's early interest in the sport. Basilio fought some bouts in the Marine Corps

Basilio

before turning professional in 1948, at the age of 21. In 1953, he decisioned Hall of Farmer Ike Williams and then defeated Billy Graham to win the New York State Welterweight Championship. After fighting Graham to a draw in a rematch the same year, Basilio faced Kid Gavilan for the Welterweight Championship of the World. Fighting in the War Memorial Auditorium in Syracuse, New York before 6,803 fans, Basilio came close to knocking out Gavilan in the second round. Gavilan, however, rose at the count of nine and prevailed in a fifteen-round decision.

Carmen Basilio in a classic pose.

Basilio got another chance to fight for the welterweight title when he faced the new champion, Tony DeMarco, in the Syracuse War Memorial Auditorium in 1955. In a wild, bloody brawl, DeMarco led through eight rounds. In the tenth, Basilio floored DeMarco twice. DeMarco managed to avoid a knockout but succumbed in the twelfth when the referee stopped the fight. Basilio lost his title to Johnny Saxton in 1956. Basilio had Saxton seriously shaken up, but the challenger's corner reportedly fabricated a delay in replacing a damaged glove, giving Saxton time to recover sufficiently to win a decision. Basilio won the rematch six months later to reclaim the title.

Basilio

In 1957, Basilio fought what many consider to be the finest battle of his career. He moved up to middleweight in a bid to topple the enduring Sugar Ray Robinson. Robinson had lost and regained the title four times, and had recently came out of a short retirement. He was thirty-seven; Basilio was thirty. The contest, later ranked the twelfth greatest fight of all time by *The Ring*, took place in Yankee Stadium before a crowd of 38,000. At the start of the fight, Robinson jabbed Basilio persistently and effectively. He bloodied Basilio's nose in the third round and cut his left eye in the fourth. Basilio dominated in the fifth and continued to press Robinson in the following rounds. There was no holding back as each fighter felt the effect of many resounding, jamming punches. At times, each man appeared dazed and ready to drop. After fifteen rounds had finally gone by, the bloody and exhausted Basilio went down on one knee to pray. A few moments later, it was announced that he had won the split decision to take the middleweight title. The rematch six months later was just as gruesome, with Basilio fighting one-eyed from the sixth round on. This time, Robinson won the decision. In three later bids, Basilio failed to claim the middleweight title from subsequent champions Gene Fullmer and Paul Pender.

Basilio's aggressive, charging style and powerful left hook enabled him to win championships in two weight classes and to have a long and memorable career. In retirement, he worked as a physical education instructor at LeMoyne College in Syracuse and as a Genesee Brewery representative. Basilio's hometown of Canastoga is also the site of the International Boxing Hall of Fame. Basilio is a frequent visitor to the shrine that honors him and other great boxers of the past.

Paz

inny Paz is known to the boxing world and to his many friends as the "Pazmanian Devil." He has had to overcome a number of obstacles and near death, but the five-time world champion has a way of bouncing back.

His career as a boxer nearly came to an end on November 14, 1991 in a car accident. With two broken bones in his neck, doctors wondered if Paz would walk again and many believed his boxing career was ended.

Soon after the accident, and with trainer Kevin Ronney at his side, Paz appeared on the Nick Manzello TV Sports Page. "I know it doesn't look good," he said. "but don't count Paz out. I'll be back." And return he did—with a bang.

Born on December 16, 1962, Paz began boxing at the age of seven and continued to lace on gloves until the age of eleven. He attended Cranston High School, in Rhode Island, where he lettered in baseball and football.

Paz had an outstanding amateur boxing career as a member of the USA's international boxing team and won his share of trophies. He thought about trying out for the 1984 Olympic team but decided to turn pro instead. He had an outstanding 100-12 record as an amateur.

Paz won his first world title on June 7, 1987 with a fifteen-round decision over reigning IBF world lightweight champion Greg Haugen in an epic war in front of a sell-out crowd at the Providence Civic Center. It would be four years before Vinny was once again a world champion. Thought of as a flash in the pan, Vinny proved to everyone that he had lasting credentials. He dominated WBA world junior middleweight champion Gilbert Dele and stopped him in the twelfth round.

Soon after the Dele fight, though, Vinny was involved in the automobile accident.

He finally made his triumphant return to the ring just over a year later capping off an unbelievable recovery. His first opponent was former WBC world super welterweight champion Luis Santana. Paz won a unanimous ten-round decision that not only marked his return to the ring, but also marked the beginning of major professional boxing at the Foxwoods Casino in Mashantucket, Connecticut.

Vinny went on to defeat top contender Brett Lally and former world champions Lloyd Honeyghan and Robbie Sims before getting another shot at a world title. This time Vinny moved on to Aspen, Colorado to take on Dan Sherry for the IBO world super middleweight title. Paz dominated the former model and took the championship via an eleventh-round knockout.

A victory over contender Jacques LeBlanc set up another world title fight. This time the bright lights of Las Vegas were the setting for Paz's fight against future Hall of Famer Roberto Duran. Vinny walked away with a twelve-round unanimous decision and the IBC world super middleweight crown. A win over contender Rafael Williams set up a return fight with Duran. This time, Vinny did battle in familiar surroundings— the Atlantic City Convention Center. Paz gave the former champion a boxing lesson and easily won a twelve-round decision to retain his IBC title.

The second win over Duran set up a shot at IBF world super middleweight champion, and pound for pound the greatest fighter in the world, Roy Jones, Jr. It was not Paz's night from the start. His fight went off an hour late, and by the time he made it to the ring he had used half of his gas tank in preparations. Still, Paz lasted longer than most of Jones' previous challengers, getting stopped in the sixth round.

Many observers thought that was the end of the line for the "Pazmanian Devil," but they were wrong again. Vinny returned one year later to take on the hot young prospect and New England rival, "Dangerous" Dana Rosenblatt. It was supposed to be WBU World Middleweight Champion Rosenblatt's coming out party on pay-per-view. Instead, it was Paz's party as he stopped his undefeated foe in the fourth round to take the WBU world super middleweight championship.

Again, Paz was out of the ring for over a year. Vinny came back on December 6, 1997 to take on former world title challenger and WBC International Super Middle Weight Champion Herol Graham in England. Graham, a crafty southpaw, chose to run rather than fight. However, the hometown judges awarded Graham a lopsided unanimous decision, a decision that *Fight Game* magazine called one of 1997's "top ten worst decisions."

In July 1998, Vinny returned to Foxwoods Casino and in front of a sell-out crowd gave an awesome performance that some journalists called the "Fight of the Year" and the "Best Fight Ever at Foxwoods."

Paz

Vinny went to war with veteran contender Glenwood Brown. Paz found himself on the mat in the third round, but all the knockdown did was motivate Vinny who scorched his slower foe to sweep the remaining rounds. In the end, Vinny had thrown and landed twice as many punches as his opponent.

Paz then rolled through a string of top fighters, defeating Pittsburgh native Arthur Allen (tenth-round unanimous decision), the World Boxing Association's twelfth-rated contender Undra White (ninth-round technical knockout), former North American Boxing Federation champion Joseph Kiwanuka (tenth-round decision), and former WBF world light heavyweight champion Esteban Cervantes (tenth-round decision). This winning streak set up the long awaited rematch with rival Dana Rosenblatt. Despite fighting with an injured right hand, Paz scored a knockdown and most thought scored a decision win, however in the end Paz dropped a very disputed decision.

Vinny returned to the ring to take on former two-time world title challenger Aaron "Superman" Davis. It just was not Paz's night as he lost the fight via an eighth-round technical knockout.

Besides being a five-time world champion, Vinny has carried himself well outside the ring. Always quick with a smile, Paz is more than happy to speak with fans and sign autographs, something that has made him a hero in his home state of Rhode Island.

Paz has said that he would not retire from the ring until he gets his fiftieth win. He would love to see number 50 come in a third bout with Rosenblatt.

While he waits and wonders when he will get a chance at 50, Paz keeps busy and continues to line up post-boxing gigs, including acting.

He will film *Thunder Doyle* with girlfriend Carrie Lane in Rhode Island. He has guest starred on an episode of "Police Academy" and has taken part in four feature films, including one with Sylvester Stallone.

Graziano

lthough Rocky Graziano often found himself embroiled in controversy during his boxing career, he emerged as one of the most popular fighters of the 1940s and early 1950s. Born Thomas Rocco Barbella, Graziano grew up on the Lower East Side of New York City. He overcame an impoverished, delinquent boyhood to become the middleweight champion of the world.

After a stint in reform school, Graziano entered the Metropolitan AAU boxing tournament in New York as a replacement for another fighter. Graziano won the tournament—his first organized boxing experience.

Graziano served time in prison at Riker's Island and later, while in the Army, in military prison for striking an officer. He officially began his professional boxing career in 1942, although he had fought so-called amateur bouts for compensation before that.

By 1945, Graziano had started to make a name for himself, knocking out Billy Arnold and Al "Bummy" Davis. In 1946, the title war between Graziano and middleweight champ Tony Zale commenced. Zale ultimately got the best of Graziano but not until Graziano had won the crown for a year. It started when Graziano challenged Zale for the championship in a fight in New York. *The Ring's* International Ratings Panel called it the fourth-greatest fight of all time. Both fighters had strong crowd appeal and the fans went crazy as Zale and Graziano traded explosive punches. Zale knocked Graziano down in the first round, then, just before the bell ended the third round, Graziano sent Zale through the ropes. Zale recovered to knockout Graziano with a left hook in the sixth.

In their rematch the next year in Chicago, Graziano got his revenge. Zale cut Graziano early and punished him severely in the third round, but Graziano recovered to knock Zale down in the sixth and then battered him at will along the ropes before the referee stopped the fight. In 1948, Zale knocked out Graziano in the third round to reclaim the title.

The Zale fights serve as prime examples of Graziano's style. A great slugger, Graziano was not a clever boxer. He absorbed a tremendous amount of punishment while he waited for the opening he needed to go for a knockout. His record of 52 knockouts in 83 fights is proof of his great punching ability.

Before the second Zale fight, the New York State Athletic Commission suspended Graziano's boxing license for failing to report an attempted bribe, so the fight was moved to Chicago. The ban was hard on Graziano, and many observers, including noted boxing writer W.C. Heinz, believed the nine-month penalty to be unduly harsh. Then, when Graziano backed out of a scheduled fight in California with former champion Fred Apostoli, he drew the ire of West Coast boxing officials.

In 1952, Graziano went up against the middleweight champion Sugar Ray Robinson for one last title attempt. In the third round, Graziano floored Robinson, but Robinson quickly recovered and knocked out Graziano before the round was finished. Graziano fought just once more before retiring.

After his retirement from boxing, he appeared in television shows and movies, exhibited his paintings in galleries, and published a popular autobiography, *Somebody Up There Likes Me*. The book was adapted into the 1956 hit movie with the same name starring Paul Newman.

In 83 professional fights, Graziano won 67 times, 52 by knockout. He lost 10 and fought 8 draws. He died on May 22, 1990.

He was elected to the National Italian American Sports Hall of Fame in 1977.

Graziano

FOOTBALL

By the time the first Italian-American superstars had donned a major league uniform, baseball was already a well-established sport with a large fan base. But during the slow ascendancy of football in this country, Italian Americans would have the opportunity to alter the very nature of the sport.

American football evolved from college rugby and soccer in the late 1800s. One of the earliest professional teams, the Latrobe Athletic Club in Pennsylvania, signed Ed Abbaticchio, a fullback in 1897. He was the first Italian-American professional football player. The journalist and former football competitor Fielding Yost credited Abbaticchio with inventing the spiral kick.

In 1897, Abbaticchio joined the Phillies as their second baseman. He was the first player to have played both professional football and baseball, as well as the first somewhat famous baseball player of obvious Italian heritage. He earned a lifetime batting average of .254 over an eight-season career, and eventually signed with the Pittsburgh Pirates, teaming up with legendary shortstop Honus Wagner to form a deadly double-play combination.

Courtesy of the Worcester Telegram & Gazette

O n February 2, 1959, the Green Bay Packers, doormats in the National Football League for several seasons, announced a new coach and general manager. Gone was former NFL player-turned-coach, Ray (Scooter) McLean. In his place was Vince Lombardi, a 46-year-old New York native who previously had only been a head coach at the high school level.

Fans in the Wisconsin city of 75,000, who lived and died with their Packers, were stunned. Indeed, most sports fans in America were hard-pressed to remember anything about the man chosen to lead Green Bay back from 1958's dismal 1-10-1 record.

The day after Lombardi was named coach, one Wisconsin newspaper reflected the dismay of the

Lombardi

Packer faithful with headlines that read: "VINCE
WHO?"

Green Bay's executive
council that selected
Lombardi after several
months of searching was
under fire from the Packer
fans and the media for
what seemed so obvious a
mistake. For over a decade
these Packer leaders seemingly had made one blun-
der after another. Now
they had selected some-
body named Lombardi to
do a task that would challenge the greatest coaches
in the land.

While Packer fans and

Courtesy of the Worcester Telegram & Gazette

Lombardi on the sideline.

sports columnists worried about the Lombardi selection, insiders
throughout pro football felt that Green Bay had
made a very wise choice. Vince Lombardi was a
superb football man who had paid his dues as a
long-time assistant and deserved to have his own
team. Paul Brown, considered one of football's
reigning geniuses, had recommended Lombardi to
the Packers. Even "Papa Bear" George Halas, had
joined in the chorus of Lombardi supporters even
though the Chicago legend rued the fact that the
new Packer coach would face his Bears.

Lombardi's stewardship as an assistant was the
major concern of the legions who felt he lacked
qualifications. Lombardi seemed to be one of those
faceless men who served others. His record spoke to
this status—three years as an aide at Fordham, five

Lombardi

seasons at West Point, and another five with the New York Giants. His only experience as a head coach was during World War II when he directed a small parochial high school in New Jersey. It seemed obvious that Vince Lombardi was not truly qualified to lead a pro football team.

At his first press conference, Lombardi seemed to confirm that his inexperience made him a questionable selection. While dynamic, energetic, and even combative, Lombardi stunned the assembled reporters by flatly predicting he would bring a league title to Green Bay within five years!

Fans shook their heads in dismay when they read Lombardi's quote in the next day's newspapers. Everyone knew the Packers were so bad that even a Paul Brown or a George Halas would need more than five years to bring them to respectability.

However, in his first season, Vince Lombardi changed the naysayers into supporters. His 1959 Packers were the surprise of the pro league with a record of 7-5-0. With success on the field, the Packer faithful returned to the fold. Lombardi won National Football League Coach of the Year honors for his turnaround of the Packers.

Thereafter, Vince Lombardi even proved himself a poor prophet. He did not need five years to produce a champion. He did it in only three seasons.

Lombardi's second Packer team won the Western Division crown. Despite outplaying the Philadelphia Eagles, they dropped a 17-13 decision in the championship game. By then, the underdog Packers had begun to catch the nation's fancy. They did things in a methodical fashion on the field. They were efficient, hard-hitting, and smartly coached. And, fans rushed to cheer this team from the league's smallest city.

With experience in the playoffs, Lombardi had refined his team to make a championship run. In 1961 they swept to another division crown and demolished the New York Giants, 37-0, in a one-sided championship game. Green Bay added "Title-town, U.S.A." to its municipal stationary and road signs. Lombardi had become a nationally-known celebrity. He had transformed a losing team comprised of castoffs, rookies, and over-the-hill veterans into football's most successful and efficient team.

In 1962, Lombardi's green and gold clad Pack came out of the west to win a second NFL title. Their victims were the Giants once again. That season, the Packers won 21 of the 22 games they played.

In 1963 and 1964, the Packers finished second and played in what was then the NFL's runner-up consolation bowl. Vince Lombardi detested this "loser's game," and threatened the Packers with damnation if they ever finished second again and forced him into the humiliation of competing for a meaningless trophy.

Lombardi's message apparently got through to his team. In 1965 they again swept the division and the NFL title. They repeated again in 1966 and added a third consecutive league crown in 1967.

Topping this unequalled string of successes were the first two Super Bowl contests against the upstart challengers of the American Football League. In 1966, Lombardi's Packers belted the Kansas City Chiefs and the next season easily demolished the Oakland Raiders. A national television audience watched these methodical victories and Lombardi's reputation as a coach was elevated to mythic levels.

"Vince Who?" of 1959 had become a national figure. When Lombardi talked on football, coaches from the professional level down to youth football stopped and listened. A flurry of books and articles appeared on Lombardi and his Packers. Vince Lombardi had become a living legend with his photograph on both national sports and news magazines.

This attention, of course, was richly deserved. Between 1959 and 1967, Lombardi had driven the Packers to an unbelievable record of 121-37-4.

Courtesy of the Worcester Telegram & Gazette

The Packers celebrate a victory over the Oakland Raiders in Super Bowl II.

Green Bay won 10 of 12 playoff games over these years. They even won 42 of the 50 preseason exhibition games they played.

Other coaches would win more games and coach more years. But, no other professional coach would cram such great success into such a few years as did Vince Lombardi at Green Bay. And no other coach, professional or college, would attract the attention of America as did Vince Lombardi in these glory years.

Lombardi and his Packers were the primary reasons for the growth of professional football's popularity in the 1960s. Buoyed both by greater television exposure and the network revenues, pro football leaped out of the shadow of college football to carve out a following of millions of fans. Green Bay's Packers had become "America's Team."

Lombardi's success cried out for media attention. He not only had become an expert on football but a quotable authority on events at the national and international level. He jumped from the sports pages to the news sections of magazines and papers with comments on race relations, integration, urban riots, hippies, the generation gap, the war in Vietnam, college student unrest, and the condition of American society.

Vince Lombardi's abilities were magically transformed to being applicable in other sectors of American life. He was a desired speaker before business executives on managing corporations. A poll of over one thousand executives in 1967 saw Lombardi chosen as "Salesman of the Year" in America. He was offered the lieutenant governor's slot on the Democratic slate in Wisconsin and his name came up as a possible gubernatorial candidate in the Dairy State.

Even Richard Nixon and his close advisors preparing for their run at the White House were attracted to the Lombardi mystique and popularity. Despite being a lifelong Democrat, Lombardi was contacted in 1967 about his interest in being Nixon's vice presidential running mate.

At the peak of his popularity, Vince Lombardi stunned America

by announcing his retirement from active coaching. He reasoned that his dual posts at Green Bay as coach and general manger were too much for one man. He would retain the front office post and his top assistant, Phil Bengston, was given the dubious job of replacing this legend.

Even before the 1968 season, Lombardi realized leaving coaching had been a mistake. He chaffed at the routine of office management. Despite having more time for his family and improving his golf game, Vince Lombardi was unhappy. Coaching and his 16 hour days had become so much a part of his life that Lombardi was a lost soul once outside this world. But, he had by his own actions boxed himself out from returning to coach the Packers. After all, it was his own selection, Bengston, that now headed the Pack. If Lombardi would again coach, it would be with a new team in another city.

Other teams certainly wanted Lombardi. All were willing to pay a pretty price in return for his services. Offers came in from Atlanta, Boston, New Orleans, Los Angeles, and Philadelphia. Lombardi could almost

Courtesy of the Worcester Telegram & Gazette

name his own salary to these suitors. Early in 1969, Vince Lombardi broke Green Bay's heart by accepting a deal from the Washington Redskins that made him coach, general manager, and a minority owner.

In comparison to his reception in Green Bay nine years before, Lombardi's arrival in Washington rivaled that of a new president about to be inaugurated. Lombardi was now the messiah that could create dynasties. Fans in the nation's capital lined up to vie for season tickets. With Lombardi they were certain Washington would be: "First in war, first in peace, and, first in the NFL!"

The Washington Redskins were a mirror of the Packers when Lombardi arrived. In 1968 under Otto Graham they had a poor 5-9-0 record. Their last winning season had been back in the 1940s. Now, with Lombardi, the miracle-worker of Green Bay, it was inevitable that the Redskins were soon to be pro football's dynasty for the 1970s.

A postage stamp honoring Vince Lombardi.

This Lombardi and Redskin dynasty was not to be. True, Lombardi did turn the team around in the 1969 season. They continued the Lombardi tradition of not having a losing season as they finished 7-5-2. This record hinted at even greater things to come.

But, within nine months of the close of the 1969 season, Vince Lombardi was dead. His last opponent was cancer that struck him early in the summer of 1970. He died on September 3, 1970, less than three months after he had been diagnosed.

Within weeks of Lombardi's passing, a second wave of "Lombardiana" poured from publishing houses. Among the first of these post-Lombardi books was Tim Dowling's *Coach: A Season with Lombardi.*

Dowling's manuscript on the 1969 Redskins and their coach was completed before Lombardi died. It had been scheduled to be published to coincide with the start of the 1970 season. A new and brief preface was added noting Lombardi's passing and the book hit bookstores only days after the coach's funeral.

In many ways, Dowling's book anticipated the later studies on Lombardi. He personally admired Lombardi but found him as a man to be enigmatic. Lombardi was "tough and ruthless," "honest and fair," had a monstrous ego but was at times "shy, uncertain, generous and compassionate."

This portrait of a man of confusing and contradictory traits and tendencies was the theme for later Lombardi books. A reason in part for this mystery about Lombardi the man was due to his practice of keeping the press at arm's-length and his tendency to parry queries with oblique replies. Questions aimed at defining the essence of the coach thus received no clarification from the man. Lombardi replied, "I've been written up as a beast . . . I don't know what I am."

Vince Lombardi, of course, knew fully well what he was, where he had come from, and what he was about. He had been created by values, beliefs, attitudes, and experiences derived from his family, schooling, his own athletic playing years, and service as a coach under other men. There were no real contradictions to Lombardi as a man or as a coach. In fact, there could be little separation of the man from the coach.

Green Bay's quarterback during the Packer's golden years, Bart Starr, once noted that Lombardi's philosophy included principles and values that some people in American society found to be corny in the 1960s. Lombardi was indeed "old-fashioned."

Courtesy of University Photo/Graphics, Pennsylvania State University

Paterno

Entering the 2001 football season Joseph Vincent Paterno was within reach of college football's holy grail. After 51 years as a college coach, 403 games, untold first downs, countless fumbles and interceptions and innumerable pressure-packed moments, Angelo and Florence Paterno's first-born was just steps away from the summit of the game's Mount Everest.

The 2001 Nittany Lions responded to their first 0-4 start in the history of the program by battling back to win five of their last seven games and push their coach's victory total to 327. Paterno passed Paul "Bear" Bryant on October 27 when the Lions secured his 324th victory by rallying from a 27-9 deficit to defeat Ohio State 29-27 in the greatest Beaver Stadium comeback under their legendary coach.

Milestones, Paterno has said, are not things that motivate him. One day he may look back on the rich canvas he has created, but it won't be anytime soon because retirement is about the last thing on his mind. He recently signed a five-year extension of his current Penn State contract and hinted he might even go beyond that term if his health permits.

"Joe Paterno stays constant," *Trenton Times* columnist Harvey Yonvener said in a column in 1999, following Penn State's Alamo Bowl victory over Texas A&M. "At 72, he's ready for the next class of dream-seekers to arrive, ready to try to lead them to 21st Century glory."

Before Paterno removes those white athletic socks and trademark black Nikes for the final time, there's not much doubt he will have established THE benchmark for college football coaches.

His total of 327 victories at the end of the 2001 season was first among his active peers. His .790 winning percentage ranked him number two in the current coaching hierarchy. His twenty bowl victories are an NCAA all-time record as is the thirty postseason appearances he has made with the Nittany Lions.

Paterno's 1999 Lions were ranked either first or second for most of the season until a nightmare three-game stretch left Penn State's national championship hopes in tatters. Despite the disappointment, the veteran coach was able to regroup his forces for an impressive 24-0 victory over Texas A&M in the Alamo Bowl, only the second postseason shutout in Penn State football history. It closed out a 10-3 campaign and was the Lions' sixth bowl victory in the past seven years.

"When it was over," one *Dallas Morning News* reporter noted in his post-Alamo Bowl account, "Penn State's 24-0 blasting of the Aggies sent a powerful message on behalf of Paterno, even if he's not one to crow about personal accomplishments. The game may pass some coaches by. It hasn't even caught up with this one."

The ten-win season placed the Nittany Lions number eleven in the final Associated Press and ESPN/*USA Today* polls. It marked the eighteenth time in thirty-four years that a Paterno-coached Penn State team won ten or more games. Three Paterno squads finished a perfect 12-0: in 1973, 1986, and 1994.

Paterno's longevity in a profession where change is a constant bor-

Courtesy of University Photo/Graphics, Pennsylvania State University

Coach Paterno in his younger days.

ders on unbelievable. Consider that since Paterno succeeded Engle as head coach in 1966 there have been 671 head coaching changes at Division I schools.

Paterno has remained true to the ideal that a university is an educational institution first and foremost, graduating his student-athletes and constantly striving to instill values of citizenship and sportsmanship.

"Joe makes a point of stressing academics over football," Bob Rickenbach, a 1970's era offensive lineman, said. "He says football can only carry you so far and he's right. There aren't many schools or coaches that take that approach."

It is well chronicled that Paterno's 1999 team included three first-team All-Americans and the first two players selected in the NFL draft. It is less well

known that it also included his 21st first-team Academic All-American and 17th NCAA Postgraduate Scholarship winner. Sixteen Nittany Lions received 1999 Academic All-Big Ten Conference recognition.

Paterno's dual focus of athletic excellence and academic accomplishment is one of the reasons the Maxwell Club of Philadelphia presented him with its eleventh annual Reds Bagnell Award for contributions to the game of football. Previous winners of the Bagnell Award include the late NFL Commissioner Pete Rozelle, Lamar Hunt of the Kansas City Chiefs, and Dan Rooney of the Pittsburgh Steelers. The only other college coaches to receive it are Eddie Robinson of Grambling State University and Bill Manlove of Widener University.

"The greatest testimonial to the Penn State football program is its list of graduates," said former All-American center Bill Lenkaitis, who is now a dentist in Foxboro, Massachusetts. "Look at where these guys are now and what they're doing. Look how many go to medical school or law school. Look how many become heads of corporations.

"That's the real test of a college football program," Lenkaitis said, "not how many trophies they have in the window, not how many players they have in the Hall of Fame, but how many guys they have making it, really making it 10 to 15 years down the road. On that score, I'd put Penn State up against any of them."

Lenkaitis' observations mirror his coach's response when asked to name his greatest team. It won't necessarily be the one with the most wins, most All-Americans, or the most postseason awards, Paterno has said. Rather, it will be the team that has yielded the most productive members of society.

Giving back is a theme Paterno not only preaches but also practices. He and his wife and their five children gave the University $3.5 million in 1998 to endow faculty positions and scholarships, and to support two building projects.

Paterno was the 1998 winner of the initial State Farm Eddie Robinson Coach of the Year Award, established to recognize the qualities of Coach Robinson as a role model to students and players, an active member of the community and an accomplished coach. The award included a handsome crystal trophy and a $10,000 cash prize to Penn State's General Scholarship Fund in Coach Paterno's name.

In 1999, Paterno received the National Heritage Award of the Anti-Defamation League at a March dinner in Philadelphia.

"Coach Paterno is an outstanding role model, mentor and leader, humanitarian, and philanthropist," ADL regional director Barry Morrison said. "He has helped build champions both on and off the field through his ongoing commitment to the values that ADL stands for—equality, dignity, educational achievement, tolerance and diversity."

" ... even though he is enormously successful at it. From the perspective of meaningful contributions to society, the least important thing Joe Paterno does is coaching football," *Philadelphia Inquirer* sports columnist Bill Lyon wrote on the occasion of the ADL Award.

"Angelo Paterno [Joe's father] died in 1955, when his son was an assistant coach, 11 years away from becoming the head coach. But his son became an idealist and jousts still with windmills, and it is difficult to believe if he had become a barrister, while he would have been a good one, that Joe Paterno would have affected as many lives, brought more good than he has as a coach."

"He's tough as hell," former All-American linebacker and former NFL standout Shane Conlan (Buffalo Bills, St. Louis Rams) said in an interview, "but he does things the way they're supposed to be done. He follows the rules. He believes you're there for an education. He teaches you more than football. He teaches you about life."

Paterno, whose tenure at Penn State—16 years as an assistant and 34 as head coach—spans the administrations of ten United States presidents, owns one of

Paterno

Courtesy of the Worcester Telegram & Gazette

Coach Paterno is carried off the field after Penn State's 27-23 victory over Georgia in the 1983 Sugar Bowl in New Orleans.

sport's most substantial resumes in his five-decade plus career in Happy Valley.

Paterno needed fewer games (246) to reach the 200-win plateau than any of the ten major college coaches on that list. He also was the quickest to achieve 300 victories. It took Bear Bryant, the previous leader, 393 games to reach that level; Paterno attained that lofty peak in 380 games.

His teams have registered seven undefeated regular seasons and twenty squads have finished in the final top ten. He has had twenty-eight teams finish in the top twenty. Penn State has won the Lambert Meadowlands Trophy, emblematic of Eastern football supremacy, twenty-one times in Paterno's coaching run.

Paterno

One of the astonishing statistics about his tenure is that he has been on the coaching staff for more than half of the football games played by the Lions since the program began in 1887.

The January 1, 1997 Fiesta Bowl was the University's 1,044th game and Paterno's 522nd since arriving on campus. He has been absent only twice for an opening kickoff—at Army in 1955 due to the death of his father and at Syracuse in 1977 when his son, David, was seriously injured in an accident.

Paterno admitted to being especially energized when the Nittany Lions, after more than 100 years as an independent, signed on as members of the Big Ten Conference in 1993. It did not take long for Penn State to flex its muscles in the new neighborhood.

In just its second year of conference affiliation, Paterno guided Penn State to a 12-0 record, including a victory in the 1995 Rose Bowl, becoming the first Big Ten team to record an undefeated season in 26 years. The Lions were ranked number two behind Nebraska in the final polls, marking the twelfth time a Paterno-led squad has finished in the top five.

Defining Joe Paterno by wins and losses, however, is to trivialize his contributions to intercollegiate athletics. This native of Brooklyn, New York, is not a man of misplaced priorities.

"How many football coaches majored in English Literature at an Ivy League school?" asked retired Penn State athletic director Jim Tarman, a Paterno friend since 1950. "When he sits up half the night, as he did for years, doing 'Xs' and 'Os' for the next day's practice or next Saturday's game, he always listens to opera. I think the fact that he has such a broad range of interests is one of the reasons our football program has been different."

Paterno always has concentrated on seeing that his student-athletes go to class, devote the proper time to studies and graduate.

"The players who have been most important to success of Penn State teams," Paterno has said, "have just naturally kept their priorities straight: football a high second, but academics an undisputed first."

The most recent NCAA report for Division I institutions revealed that the Penn State football program had a graduation rate of 76.5 percent for the entering class of 1993-94.

In his extraordinary career, Penn State has produced at least one first-team All-American 31 times. More than 225 of his players have signed with National Football League teams and 25 have been first-round draft choices. Defensive end Courtney Brown (selected by the Cleveland Browns) and linebacker LaVar Arrington (selected by the Washington Redskins) were the top two picks in the 2000 NFL draft, only the third time in the history of the modern draft that the first two players chosen have been college teammates.

In a 1995 survey of pro football general managers and personnel directors by *The Sporting News*, Penn State was the clear-cut winner as the college program that best prepares players for the NFL.

"That program is well-rounded from the standpoint that Joe Paterno demands discipline from his players, both academically and on the field," former Chicago Bears director of player personnel Rod Graves said. "Standards of character are very high there. The kids practice extremely hard. I don't care whether you are bringing in a free agent or a first-round draft choice, those kids know how to work. Nine times out of ten you'll never have any problem with those kids off the field."

Significant as it is, Paterno's football portfolio offers but a glimpse of his multi-faceted personality. He has taken on duties away from the field with the same sense of purpose and ambition.

The Paternos have won wide admiration for their philanthropy. Their more than $4 million in gifts, in conjunction with their volunteer service to Penn State, make the Paternos a unique couple among colleges and universities nationwide. Their pledge is believed to be the most generous gift ever made by a collegiate coach and his family to a university.

"I have a theory that Joe coaches not so much for what he can do for football as for what he can do for the university and the community," Penn State president Graham Spanier said. "And that makes me the luckiest university president in the country."

The Paternos' effort as co-chairs of the campaign to expand Pattee Library included a personal contribution of $250,000 among the $14

Courtesy of University Photo/Graphics, Pennsylvania State University

Coach Paterno surveys the field.

million raised. The Penn State Board of Trustees voted to name the new library wing after the Paternos. The five story, 127,000-square foot expansion doubled the size of Pattee Library.

Paterno was also a major contributor of both money and time to the $352 million campaign for Penn State, for which he served as Vice Chair. He also is an honorary chair for the University's $1 billion Grand Destiny Campaign. He and his wife established the Paterno Libraries Endowment in 1984 with gifts totaling $120,000. Subsequent contributions have pushed the Endowment's total to $4 million.

"I've said it a hundred times," Paterno stated at the time the drive began, "a great library is the heart of a great university, and if we want to remain a big-league university, we've got to have a big-league library."

"Sue and Joe Paterno are legendary at this institution, not only because of the notable and consistent success of the Nittany Lions, but also because of the values they have espoused over the years," former president Joab Thomas said at the time the Board of Trustees' decision was announced to name the new library wing after the first family of Penn State football.

"Family, learning, loyalty and commitment are prominent among those values. This new library will stand as an appropriate tribute to all that they have done for Penn State."

Paterno also was a donor and committee member on the campaign to build the Bryce Jordan Center and has committed $250,000 to the drive to construct an All-Sports Museum, which is a part of the Beaver Stadium expansion project.

The icon of college coaching has elevated Penn State football to a level matched by only a very few. And, since the day he arrived on the campus as a fresh-faced assistant on Rip Engle's new staff, Paterno has proven winning and educating are not mutually exclusive goals.

Another former player, All-American offensive lineman Dave Joyner, was elected to the GTE/COSIDA Academic All-American Hall of Fame in 1991. Joyner, an orthopedic surgeon who served as a physician for the 1992 United States Winter Olympic Games team, was the first Penn Stater to do so.

"His primary interest in his football players is as members of society," Dr. Joyner said. "He wanted you to be outstanding individuals in everything you did, not just as football players."

Joyner is among the 55 first-team All-Americans Paterno has developed at Penn State. Two of his many NFL players—linebacker Jack Ham and fullback Franco Harris—have been enshrined in the Pro Football Hall of Fame. Ham, defensive tackle Mike Reid, tight end Ted Kwalick, linebacker Dennis

Onkotz and running back John Cappelletti are members of the National Football Foundation College Football Hall of Fame.

While personal Hall of Fame consideration awaits his retirement, one of Paterno's honors testifies to his uniqueness.

In December 1991, Paterno became the first active coach ever to receive the National Football Foundation and College Football Hall of Fame Distinguished American Award. The award was instituted in 1966.

Other past winners include General James Van Fleet, Hollywood personalities Bob Hope and the late Jimmy Stewart, Notre Dame president Theodore Hesburgh, the late NFL Commissioner Pete Rozelle, and captains of industry such as John Galbreath, Sonny Werblin and the late Leon Hess. Two deceased former coaches—Vince Lombardi and Dave Nelson—are previous winners, although neither was actively coaching when honored. Tom Osborne of Nebraska received the award in 1995, then the second active coach to be cited.

Not necessarily presented on an annual basis, the award is made on those occasions when a person emerges "who over a long period of time has exhibited leadership and who has made significant contributions to the betterment of amateur football in America."

Paterno

Then President George Bush, honored with the Foundation's Gold Medal on the same evening, said in a letter to the more than 1,000 guests at New York's Waldorf-Astoria Hotel:

"Throughout his tenure at Penn State, Joe Paterno has led his Nittany Lions in smart, aggressive, team-oriented football. As their plain white jerseys and blue numbers attest, they're not a flashy bunch. But at the conclusion of each collegiate season, they're invariably among the top teams in the country. Most importantly, at the end of their college careers Joe's players have learned those valuable lessons of character and moral conduct that typify Coach Paterno himself."

Another former president, Ronald Reagan, characterized Paterno as a person "who has never forgotten that he is a teacher who's preparing his student not just for the season, but for life."

As one almost could expect, Paterno sees his role as larger than merely charting "Xs" and "Os" on a chalkboard.

"What are coaches?" Paterno asked in his acceptance speech at the 1991 Hall of Fame dinner. "Number one, we're teachers and we're educators. We have the same obligations as all teachers at our institutions, except we probably have more influence over our young people than anyone other than their families.

" . . . we're dealing with emotions; we're dealing with commitment; we're dealing with discipline, and loyalty and pride. The things that make a difference in a person's life—pride, loyalty and commitment—are the things that make a difference in this country. We're teaching them the realities of the competitive life."

Endorsement of Paterno's methods was apparent in a 1995 survey of college football by *Newsday*, which listed him number one as "the best head coach at preparing his team for Saturday" and credited him with running "the best program in the country."

The kind of success the Lions have achieved has not blurred Paterno's vision of what is right about college athletics.

"Just winning is a silly reason to be serious about a game," he said in his autobiography, *Paterno: By the Book*. "For a kid still in school, devotion to winning football games at nearly any cost may cripple his mind for life. Institutions of higher learning don't have the moral right to exploit and mislead inexperienced kids that way.

"The purpose of college football is to serve education," Paterno said, "not the other way around. I hound my players to get involved. Ten years from now I want them to look back on college as a wonderful time of expanding themselves—not just four years of playing football."

Paterno's support of scholarship and his creative and compelling views on sports and education have been widely recognized. He has been a frequent wit-

ness at Congressional hearings and he appeared before the Knight Commission. He delivered the Penn State spring commencement address in 1973 and is the recipient of three honorary degrees— Doctor of Laws from Brown, Doctor of Humane Letters from Gettysburg College and Doctor of Laws from Allegheny College.

In 1991, Paterno was inducted as an honorary member of the Penn State chapter of Eta Sigma Phi, the national classics society, which honors excellence in the study of the ancient Greeks and Romans.

"We wanted to honor him for two reasons," Michele Ronnich, a classics professor said. "For the wonderful library fund he established . . . and also for his abiding love of Virgil. I don't imagine there is another football coach in the country who can say that he's read the *Aeneid* in Latin and loved it. He is truly unique."

In February of 1994, Paterno received the Ernie Davis Award, presented by the Leukemia Society of America and named in honor of the late Syracuse All-American and Heisman Trophy winner. Paterno was the first coach to receive the award, which honors football players and coaches who actively serve mankind and strive for academic and athletic excellence.

The Sons of Italy Foundation awarded Paterno its National Education and Leadership Award in May of 1996. In February 1997, Michigan State University, one of Penn State's colleagues in the Big Ten Conference, presented its prestigious Duffy Daugherty Memorial Award, named for the Spartans' legendary late head coach to Paterno "in recognition of his outstanding contributions to college football."

Paterno received the Vince Lombardi Foundation Coach of the Year Award presented by the Lombardi Foundation in March 1998, for "service to college football."

With his success has come a certain celebrity, which Paterno tolerates although he often finds it disruptive to his coaching persona.

He is widely sought as a speaker for clinics and

banquets and has appeared in magazine, newspaper and radio/television advertisements for companies like Milano Bread, Bell of Pennsylvania, Burger King and American Express. He has been generous with his time to charitable causes as well. He and his wife, Sue, have been heavily involved with the Pennsylvania Special Olympics, held annually in June on the Penn State campus.

Paterno was the first football coach ever named by *Sports Illustrated* as its Sportsman of the Year. His 1986 selection marked only the second time a college coach was cited for the honor (UCLA basketball coach John Wooden was the first.)

Paterno had another unique experience in the summer of 1992 when he attended the dedication of the "Joe Paterno Child Development Center" on the Beaverton, Oregon, Campus of Nike, Inc. Nike said Paterno's "career demonstrates that a teacher's caring concern for each student's development is the key to unlocking each student's potential."

His "folk hero" reputation in Central Pennsylvania has spawned an entire line of Paterno products, including coffee mugs (Cup of Joe), life size cardboard cutouts (Stand-up Joe), the Paterno bean bag buddy, JoePa Christmas Ornaments and golf balls with his familiar face ("like the Penn State offense, three out of four guaranteed to go up the middle").

The life-size cutout shows up at wedding receptions, birthday and anniversary parties and nearly was in a police lineup. Startled by a silhouette in the house of vacationing neighbors, a high school student summoned police, who surrounded the house, only, upon entering, to find the "prowler" was a Stand-up Joe.

Paterno has written two books—*Football My Way* with Gordon White and the late Merv Hyman and *Paterno: By the Book* with Bernie Asbell—and at least three others have been written about him—*The Paterno Legacy* with the staff of *Pittsburgh Post-Gazette*; *No Ordinary Joe* by Michael O'Brien and *Quotable Joe*, a compilation of quotes by and about him by L. Budd Thalman.

Paterno's thick glasses, rolled-up pant legs and white athletic socks have become signatures every bit as familiar to the Penn State faithful as the McDonald's golden arches or the Nike swoosh. So, too, are the Nittany Lions' conservative uniforms, with the high-top black shoes, white helmets bereft of logos, and plain jerseys without the players' names on the back.

"I don't think our uniforms look that bad," he once said. "I think they say something to kids about team-oriented play and an austere approach to life."

Born on the 18th Street in Brooklyn, on December 21, 1926, Paterno remembers his old neighborhood as a place where "playing daily at sports was our work, not only touch football but also punch ball and stickball . . . "

Paterno went to St. Edmond's Grammar School and Brooklyn Prep High School where he played as a senior on the best Catholic-school team in the city. Brooklyn Prep's only loss was to St. Cecilia of Englewood, New Jersey, coached by a young Vince Lombardi.

The late Father Thomas Bermingham, one of his high school teachers, recalled, "I had a sense that this young man had read far beyond his years and was still reading on his own. I called him after

class and I said, 'Joseph, I can't make you but I would love to have you do much more than the rest of the class.' And typical Joe Paterno, he jumped at the chance."

From Brooklyn Prep, Paterno, after serving the final year of World War II in the U.S. Army, accepted an athletic scholarship to Brown University.

Courtesy of the Worcester Telegram & Gazette

The 1924 Georgetown team, Coach Lou Little's first, lost to Bucknell 14-6, a game they should have won. At the following Monday's practice, Coach Little was seething, and when he got around to the Hoya center, Jerry Minihan, he crescendoed.

"Minihan," Coach Little roared, "take off that uniform and never put it on again!"

Jerry Minihan, later the Very Reverend Jeremiah F. Minihan, auxiliary bishop of Boston, was by nature respectful of appropriate authority. Instead of reporting to Tuesday's practice, he attended a vaudeville show in Washington. That night, Coach Little confronted him.

"Where were you today?" he demanded.

"I went to a show," Minihan replied. "You told me to take off the uniform and never put it on again."

Little contemplated the young man querulously.

"Don't you know better than to pay attention to me when I'm mad?" he asked.

"Mister Coach," replied Jerry, "when you're mad, I pay strict attention."

Minihan was back in uniform on Wednesday, and as Little gained in coaching experience, his rages decreased. But his authority was never questioned.

Nor his devotion to football. Any thought unrelated to the game didn't distract him for long, not even the contemplation of a full-course dinner at Mamma Leone's; he was a stalwart at table.

"Lou came to my first public Mass in Haverhill, Massachusetts, July 27, 1930," Bishop Minihan said as he smiled. "Father Jerry Graham was my archpriest, whose duties may be likened to a prompter's. Actually, I didn't need one, because I'd been saying Mass in Rome for seven months before returning to the States. Well, after that first Mass in Haverhill, Lou walked with me to my house. 'Jerry,' he asked, 'who was that white-haired man beside you on the altar?'

" 'That was my parish priest, my archpriest for the Mass,' I said, and explained the reason for the archpriest. Lou listened and then shook his head.

" 'He never should have been there—he was blocking the interference all through the Mass.' "

If Lou Little had the material to work with the last twenty years of his career that he had the first thirteen, he might well have ranked among the first twenty-five coaches in all-time winning percentage. His six seasons at Georgetown (1924-29) show a record of 39-12-2; his first seven at Columbia (1930–36) 43-15-3; 13-season total: 82-27-5.

Through most of the 1920s and 1930s, he was recognized for what he was given: "a fair field and no favor," a coach capable of meeting the best of his contemporaries on even terms. Two of his Georgetown and five of his Columbia teams lost only one game. From 1931 through 1934, his record at Columbia, 29-4-2, ranked near the top.

After 1936, except for the post-World War II seasons of 1945, '46 and '47, his Columbia teams were almost invariably out manned by opponents. They had only five winning seasons in 20 for a record of 67-101-7, .403, with the last nine seasons the worst, 26-53-1, .331.

The contrast of Little's record up through 1936 with the two decades that followed provides ultimate proof of an ancient truism: No coach can make chicken salad out of chicken feathers.

In the good days, Little's teams perpetrated several dramatic upsets in settings that captured headline attention. At Georgetown they included the 1926 defeat of Syracuse, 13-7, spoiling Syracuse's undefeated season; the 7-2 triumph over the 1928 New York University team led by the brilliant back Ken Strong; and the 1929 scoreless tie with Navy. In his second season at Columbia in 1931, the Lions hung a 19-6 shocker on Dartmouth, which had run over them the year before, 52-0; it was the Lions' first over the Indians since 1899.

The game that Lou Little and Columbia football will always be remembered for, however, was the upset of a heavily favored Stanford team in the Rose Bowl, New Year's Day, 1934.

No game better exemplifies how the fate of a team and a coach in much of its context is worked out beyond their control. Columbia began that fourth season under Little, 1933, with a strong starting eleven, a few good substitutes, and a self-belief stemming from two 7-1-1 seasons back to back.

In their third game, the Lions played at Princeton, then in its second season under Fritz Crisler. This was a good but predominantly sophomore Tiger team; although it would make a perfect 9-0 record, the schedule was not too taxing. The 1933 Princeton team was by no means equal to the perfect-record team of two seasons later, when the sophomores were seniors. The season before, 1932, Columbia had defeated the Tigers 20-7. Perhaps overconfidence played a part, but Princeton won emphatically, 20-0.

At no time during the season, however, did anybody even think of the Columbia Lions for the Rose Bowl. Princeton, Army, Duke, and Pittsburgh were the Pasadena favorites. But the Big Three ban against postseason games eliminated the Princeton Tigers, the undefeated Cadets were beaten in their last game by Notre Dame,

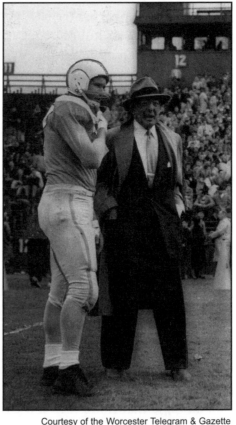

Courtesy of the Worcester Telegram & Gazette

Coach Little on the sidelines.

13-12, and Duke was defeated by Georgia Tech, 6-0. And Pittsburgh, defeated only by Minnesota, 7-3, and probably the East's best, had lost on all three of its Rose Bowl adventures, the last two to Southern California, 47-14 and 35-0.

Still, Columbia entered the minds of nobody except the people who counted: Stanford and the Rose Bowl committee. When the invitation came it was a major upset in itself. Everybody was happy for the Lions—and sorry for them. While the faculty was deciding whether the bid would be accepted, Lou Little held court to some newspapermen, including John Kieran, the erudite and readable sports columnist of *The New York Times* and celebrated pundit on the radio show "Information Please," before turning to a career as author-naturalist. Kieran described the scene in some of his neat verse:

> *The Eastern coach, with all his staff, was*
> > *Standing in the hall,*
> *The Rose Bowl bid was in, and they were*
> > *Waiting for the call,*
> *The faculty was huddling and the Dean still*
> > *Held the ball.*
> *"If twenty men were used against eleven on*
> > *their side,*
> *Do you suppose," the Head Coach said, "that*
> > *Stanford could be tied?"*
> *"I doubt it," groaned an aide-de-camp, and*
> > *broke right down and cried.*
> *"If all our men wore armor plate with rivets at*
> > *the seam,*
> *We still might save the lives of all the players on*
> > *our team,"*
> *The Head Coach said. But that seemed just a*
> > *hopeful Eastern dream.*
> *Then rose a wailing, warning voice the coaching*
> > *staff amid,*
> *"From fire and from pestilence please keep the*
> > *East safe hid,*
> *From famine and from slaughter and from*
> > *Bowl of Roses Bid."*

When the West Coast heard that Columbia had been invited and had accepted, derisive howls arose about Stanford playing "a high school team." For once, Rose Bowl tickets moved slowly, and the usual sellout would have been unlikely, even in good weather. Heavy rains forced the use of fire engine

pumps to drain off the gridiron the day before the game. Stanford coach Claude (Tiny) Thornhill suggested a postponement. Little, however, insisted the game be played; he was aware of the traditional values of "General Mud" as equalizer.

Stanford's "Vow Boys" of 1933, '34, and '35 had vowed they would never lose to Southern California, and they never did. Along the way, they also won three straight Pacific Coast Conference titles and Rose Bowl bids, losing to Alabama at Pasadena as juniors, and as seniors defeating Southern Methodist. They included many players of All-America caliber: fullback Bobby Grayson, end Monk Moscrip, tackle Bob Reynolds, and halfback Bones Hamilton. They had lost in 1933 to Washington, 6-0, been tied by Northwestern, 0-0, and had scraped through against UCLA and Santa Clara, 3-0 and 7-0.

They were not the team they would be as juniors or seniors, and may not have been ready for a top-level Bowl assignment, a factor no doubt in the selection of Columbia. None of this dilutes in the slightest the Columbia accomplishment. Stanford, the bigger, deeper, more talented team, with a two-year All-America guard in Bill Corbus, was a heavy favorite and deserved to be.

If Stanford was overconfident, it was not for long. From the opening kickoff, "the high school team" out of New York laid the wood to them. Part of the Lions' strategy rested on confidence in their defense, and a decision not to risk interceptions and field position by passing—they threw only two passes.

Throughout the first quarter, Columbia controlled the ball with quarterback Cliff Montgomery, a fine runner and passer, and fullback Al Barabas, a powerful, speedy runner, making good dents in the large Cardinal line. In the second quarter, following a punt and a five-yard penalty against Stanford, the Lions were deployed at midfield. On first down, Montgomery threw one of the two passes for the day. Star end Tony (Red) Matal made a leaping catch at the Stanford 20 and skidded three more yards. On first down from the 17, Barabas fumbled and recovered for loss of half a yard.

Now came the coup de grace. Columbia's offense, a single wing behind an unbalanced line, featured a series of tricky spinner-reverses to another back off tackle, also to the weak side.

On the play, Montgomery, taking the center snap, executed a full spin. On the first half of the spin, away from the line, he fed the ball to Barabas reversing behind him from fullback. On the second half of the spin, toward the line, he faked feeding the ball forward to right halfback Ed Brominski, who faked a slant over the weak-side tackle. The key to success was the ability of Barabas to hide the ball by holding it in his left hand against his left leg, and the ability of Brominski to convince the enemy that he actually had the ball. Both rated Oscars.

The play is essentially a flimflam. No matter how well executed or hidden, it cannot work if the defensive right end and right linebacker "play the man," which in later-day semantics has come to be known, because it sounds more scholarly, as "reading the play." Stanford's right end and right halfback were bamboozled. Barabas raced into the end zone as unopposed as if it were a signal drill. A San Francisco scribe described it nicely by quoting from John 18:40: "Now Barabas was a robber."

However, Stanford was a team easier to fool than to discourage. The infuriated Palo Altoans dominated the second half, but Little's light Blue Line from Little Old New York, though bending often to the fury of the storm, refused to snap. Six times the Indians threatened to score. Six times they were repulsed, thrice within the 20, thrice within the 10. Once they had first down on the 3; after four shots they were still a yard shy. As the clock ran out, Grayson and Hamilton made one mad, furious last attempt, but could not penetrate beyond the 10—and one of the darkest dark horses of all time had locked the favorite in the barn.

What a victory! Even Fordham's sports publicity

director—no Columbia enthusiast he—listening by radio in New Haven 3,000 miles away, had to thrill in the plucky Lions. He went so far as to sing a chorus of *Roar, Lion, Roar*, which within the hour was suddenly becoming the hit of the week at every notch on the dial. And bard Kieran once more dipped his nifty quill to speak for everybody:

> *Lou—meaning Coach Little—this lightens my fate,*
> *And this is the lilt that enlivens my song:*
> *It's bright to be right, but this time I must state,*
> *I laughed with delight when you proved I was wrong.*

As the years went on, the many staunch defensemen of the Columbia line that historic wet day were forgotten; for such is the fate of linemen.

The legerdemain that wove the heady chaplet of laurel—the play known as KF-79—seemed destined for a time to match Abraham Lincoln in belonging to the ages. It became as well known in the thirties and even into the forties as TNT, NTG, FDR, and LS/MFT. For fifteen years it reappeared regularly on sports pages, especially New York's, like a vampire violating the sundown rule.

Fourteen years after, at Baker Field, home gridiron of Columbia, a Little team pulled off his number two all-time shocker. An end named Bill Swiacki made several catches that had to be seen to be disbelieved for a 21-20 comeback upset that ended a 32-game undefeated string by Red Blaik's Army team.

Little, an outstanding football coach, was even more proficient in the field of public relations. He had an instinct for it, firmed on a keen understanding of people, and was guided also by a true expert in the field, Bob Harron, Columbia sports information director and justifiably one of the best-loved men in sports. Little on his own, however, was a Dale Carnegie incarnate.

Who else could have lasted on a coaching job through a 20-year record of 67-101-7 and only five winning seasons? Little did more than survive. He commanded a press that for consistency and elegance was the envy of many winning coaches.

It was made possible basically because Little served under two Columbia presidents, whose approach to football should serve as models: Dr. Nicholas Murray Butler, who headed the school from 1902 to 1945, and his successor, President of the United States, General of the Armies, Dwight David Eisenhower.

The doctor and the general, of course, did not account for Little's splendid press through long years of defeat. The writers deserve a salute also, for recognizing that he was doing all that could be done. This was not a consideration, however, that they accorded other coaches who were just as able but had come upon sparse days.

Little himself was mainly responsible.

At first, though, he was a good front man only on the field. He was a rough-cut youngster, the son of a successful Leominster, Massachusetts contractor, who moved from Lou's birthplace, Boston, when the coach was only four. By his own admission, Little was an indifferent scholar, interested only in sports. Failing to qualify for Yale, he went to Vermont, where his tackle play attracted attention and resulted in his transferring to Pennsylvania. At Penn, he considered studying dentistry but became convinced it was not a profession for left-handers.

Between outstanding football seasons at Penn in 1916 and 1919, Little served with distinction as a lieutenant of infantry in the Meuse-Argonne and was promoted to captain. After graduation from Penn in 1920, he played professional football for four years and sold bonds. All the time he was soaking up knowledge of the game that fascinated him, and in 1924 he was hired by Georgetown.

Except for an occasional lapse into profanity on the field, which came as a sharp contrast to his reproving "Oh, my, my, my, my, my," the later-day Little by contrast became a gruffly urbane diplomat, his pince-nez perched on his great beak giving him the mien of an erudite and amiable eagle.

Little made a tremendous initial impact, and sustained it, the kind of man few would not turn to for a second look. Big and well built, he kept himself in excellent condition by handball, golf, and gardening at his summer home in Barnstable on Cape Cod. Occasionally, he indulged himself in a cigarette or beer, and he tried to balance his gourmand feasts with periods of dieting.

Lou loved clothes. His sartorial depth—forty suits, hats, and coats, dozens of shoes, hundreds of shirts, and perhaps 500 ties, many of them strictly psychedelic.

It was not the façade, however, that won and kept writers friendly. He went out of his way to help them. It was in the early thirties that the long trip uptown to Columbia, Fordham, NYU, and Manhattan to cover football practice led to the formation of the first weekly football writers luncheons, soon to become a national habit.

To sportswriters who did favorable pieces, and they were the only kind, Lou usually dispensed thank-you notes. If a young

writer made the long trip to a Baker Field practice, Little would not only improve his education in the game but usually invite him to have supper at the training table, which featured succulent steaks. Lou even carried his good-will campaign to the extreme of tendering the writer the extra steak.

In all this communication, he drove home to the writers the high academic caliber of Columbia.

"When you have a squad, sixty percent of which are studying to be engineers, doctors, lawyers, architects, you simply must take an interest in it. Their primary purpose in college is academic development. Football must be subordinated to that purpose."

Columbia's recruiting, handled not by Little but by emissaries, allocated only part-time aid to twenty varsity and ten freshman players in a given year out of Columbia's then total of 300 available scholarships.

Blue-chippers were few. Usually, Little had a superior quarter-back-passer—Sid Luckman, Paul Governali, Gene Rossides. And he was one of the best of all coaches at developing the quarter-back in every phase.

Despite his appreciation of Columbia's philosophy and a $17,500 salary, tops for the time, Little more than once became fed up with the lack of material and was severely tempted to take one of the many offers tendered him. In 1944 the New York Yankees pro team of the old All-America Conference asked him to be coach and general manager for $25,000 plus five percent of the profits, and the Brooklyn Dodgers, of the National Football League, made an even better offer.

The only time Little seriously considered leaving Columbia, however, came after the 1947 season when Howie Odell resigned at Yale to coach at Washington. At the time Little had put togeth-er the only successful segment of his last 20 years, post-World War II seasons of 8-1, 6-3, and 7-2.

He envisioned that at fifty-four he would have to move now, if he was ever to move, and he let Yale know he was interested. Yale sparked to the idea. Columbia alumni, hearing about it, prevailed on General Eisenhower, newly appoint-ed president but not yet in office at Columbia, to call Lou to Washington and talk him out of it. Ike did, and Lou stayed. One cynical coach commented, "It would not have been surprising if, to keep Uncle Lou at Columbia, and all right with the world, uni-versity trustees had asked Pope Pius XII to dispense a special papal bull."

The patience, the mental stamina that Little demonstrated in living with losing for so long were matched by his physical fortitude. During the 1942 game that Columbia, outpersonneled, lost to Navy in the last minute, 13-9, Little shouted himself so raw that he injured his larynx. Surgery removed part of the organ, and reduced the booming roar, once a hallmark, to a painful rasp.

The last football game Little ever coached, he won, when Columbia concluded its 1956 season by beating Rutgers at New Brunswick, New Jersey, 18-12. Among those who congratulated the maestro in the locker room were four players from his first team, the 1924 Georgetown Hoyas: Frank Murray, Andy Gaffey, Eddie Brooks, and Bishop Jerry Minihan. He had not known they were there and was deeply touched. Tears filled the eyes of Lou Little, born Luigi Piccolo, as he gave each of them the Roman man's greeting of true friendship and deep affection—the baccio Romana.

Little

Courtesy of the University of Notre Dame

I n the spring of 1940, Coach Frank Leahy was putting the frosting on his Sugar Bowl champions at Boston College. A few miles away in West Springfield, Angelo Bertelli was the talk of New England prep circles.

Bertelli could play hockey. The Boston Bruins wanted him.

Bertelli could play baseball. Both the St. Louis Cardinals and the Detroit Tigers wanted him.

Most of all, Bertelli could throw a football for Notre Dame—thanks to the missionary zeal of Milton Piepul, 1940 captain and fullback of the Fighting Irish who preceded Angelo at Cathedral High.

Leahy dispatched his backfield coach and chief talent scout, Ed McKeever, who reputedly could sell

Bertelli

Florida oranges in California. It was astonishing how many boys went to Boston College after a few minutes of conversation with McKeever.

Bertelli feared a similar few minutes would be Indiana's loss and Massachusetts' gain. The evening McKeever called at the Bertelli homestead, Angelo hid by going to a downtown movie house where he sat through a double feature and two Mickey Mouse cartoons.

McKeever went back to Boston empty-handed. Bertelli entered Notre Dame, and the wheel of football fortune spun crazily. Elmer Layden resigned as Notre Dame coach to become commissioner of the National Football League. Frank Leahy returned to his alma mater to succeed Layden, and McKeever accompanied him to Notre Dame. On the first afternoon of 1941 spring practice, McKeever, still hot on the scene after stalking his man from the rock-ribbed coasts of Massachusetts to the flat prairies of Indiana, sighted his quarry.

McKeever closed in stealthily and tapped Angelo on the shoulder and inquired, "Doctor Bertelli, I presume?"

Leahy and McKeever finally had come into undisputed possession of Bertelli. It was a disillusioning experience. Angelo had a

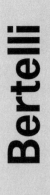

nice smile, blue eyes, brown hair, surprisingly Nordic features, but he was six feet one inch tall and weighed only 168 pounds—just three more than he had scaled in high school.

Outside of throwing a fast, accurate pass, any resemblance between Bertelli and a Notre Dame halfback was coincidental and probably an optical illusion. Angelo could punt forty yards, with a stiff wind behind him. He could run—but not far; somebody always tackled him without much trouble. Angelo didn't really run, he skated along, ankles close to the ground, no high knee action, a hangover from his hockey training.

Only a prophet could have predicted that in the fall, "Skinny" Bertelli, the awkward freshman, would pitch the Irish to an unbeaten season. Leahy was no prophet. He dropped Bertelli to the fourth team and forgot about him—for almost two weeks.

But Angelo quickly graduated from the fourth team. He received very special attention from his old friend McKeever. Each afternoon they went off into a far corner of the field and for hours practiced forward passing. Bertelli fired ball after ball with his peculiar feinting motion, flicking the ball around under his nose the way a bartender handles a cocktail shaker. You couldn't guess when or where he was going to throw.

May 1, 1941 was moving day for Angelo. The inevitable happened. Leahy promoted him to first team left halfback, a passing position in the offense that Notre Dame was using. It was inevitable that Angelo would be promoted to the first team. Anybody in West Springfield, Massachusetts would have foreseen that, for back home Angelo had reduced to a fine art the old American custom of starting in at the bottom and working to the top. Here is the bare outline of a story that would have kept Horatio Alger writing for 300 pages:

Angelo's mother and father were tobacco farmers near Venice, Italy. In 1915, they immigrated to West Springfield. Angelo's father went to work as a gas maker. The Bertelli's had three children: Rose, born in 1918; Josephine born in 1919; and Angelo, born in 1921. When Angelo was five years old, the Bertelli's returned to Venice to sell their farm and visit friends. They stayed a while, then sailed for New York, disregarding the strident protest of young Angelo, who wanted to become a gondolier.

Angelo entered West Springfield grade school, played baseball, football, and hockey—mostly hockey. He was a rink rat for the Springfield professional team. He sharpened skates, cleaned uniforms, and stayed late with the janitor to sweep up after the crowds had gone home. The players liked Angelo and taught him the tricks of the game, and he had no trouble making his high-school team. Eddie Shore, the ex–Bruins star, who later owned and managed the Springfield Indians, called Angelo the greatest prep player he ever saw.

Angelo was on the fourth team of the football squad at Cathedral High at the beginning of his junior year, until coach Billy Wise saw him fire a pass with the same wrist flick he used to bewilder goalkeepers and throw runners out at second base. Wise, who had pitched Holy Cross to football victories over Harvard in 1925 and 1926 knew a natural passer when he saw one.

Courtesy of the University of Notre Dame

Bertelli demonstrates the jump pass.

Wise showed Angelo a few tricks—how to feint and fake, look one way and throw another—and then assigned Angelo to the first team as left halfback. Angelo showed his appreciation by pitching Cathedral to eight consecutive victories and an unbeaten season.

In his senior year, he led Cathedral to eight more victories and another unbeaten season. He was named captain and quarterback of the all-city team. He graduated with honors and was president of his class.

Practice makes perfect was the secret of Angelo's hometown triumphs, and he did not forget the magic formula at Notre Dame. Leahy might have been satisfied with Angelo's passing proficiency in 1941 spring practice but Angelo was not.

Bertelli got a job painting on campus for the summer. All summer long, Angelo painted and toughened his right arm. He painted everything from the stadium press box to the apartment of Clashmore Mike, Notre Dame's Irish terrier mascot. And every afternoon George Murphy, varsity right end who lived in South Bend, drove out from town for a game of catch.

How much these practice sessions helped was apparent when Notre Dame played Georgia Tech at Atlanta. Bertelli made one of his few bad throws of the season, a wobbler seemingly destined for the bleachers close behind the end zone. Up went Murphy in the far right corner to take the ball in one hand. Up popped a big white "6" under Notre Dame on the scoreboard.

In 1913, two other Notre Dame greats, Gus Dorais and Knute Rockne, did the same thing when they spent the summer as life-guards at Cedar Point, Ohio, throwing a football around in their spare time. Then that fall they went east and forward-passed Army dizzy.

Bertelli and Murphy were rewarded, too. Murphy was elected captain for 1942, and the extra measure of passing accuracy Angelo achieved made him the most highly publicized soph-omore in the history of football.

It was a well-deserved distinction. Angelo complet-ed 70 of 123 passes for 1,027 yards. He threw eight touchdowns and set up seven others out of Notre Dame's 28 total. The Irish won eight games and tied Army for their first undefeated season since 1930. Bertelli, though only a sophomore, was runner-up to Minnesota's Bruce Smith for the Heisman Trophy.

Here was success with a capital S. It might have increased the size of Angelo's hatband, except for sev-eral reasons. Angelo could remember back to when he was a rink rat, and Angelo's teammates never let him forget that good little sophomores were seen and not heard and spoke only when spoken to.

A few days after Angelo made his victory debut against Arizona by completing 11 out of 14 passes, the inevitable ribbing of the sophomore sensation started with Steve Juzwik, Angelo's running mate at halfback, as the chief ribber. Steve discovered that Bertelli was interested in gangster lore, a sinister hobby that ran the gamut from the James boys to the Dillinger mob.

Angelo soon won the nickname of "Duke," after the comic-strip villain who was then fighting a losing battle with Dauntless Dick Tracy.

Everywhere Duke went, a few members of the Irish varsity team tagged along, slouching in the approved Humphrey Bogart manner, their hands in their pockets on imaginary guns. This pantomime brought Bertelli to the attention of the student body. Bertelli, up until now, had been merely a name in football headlines to the great majority of Notre Dame's 3,000 students.

Discovering Bertelli's identity did not exactly uplift student morale. He didn't look like much without his shoulder pads. There is the story of the freshman who got a good look at Angelo, then went out and canceled his two-dollar bet on the Northwestern game.

Gradually the ribbing shifted from the Duke's underworld interests to his clumsy running. Angelo was completing more than 50 percent of his passes, but all he heard from his teammates was the dismal news that he was averaging 1.4 yards as a ball carrier.

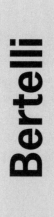

Before the Army game, Juzwik was looking out of the dressing room window in New York's Yankee Stadium. The rain was splattering down. The field was ankle-deep in mud. It was apparent that Angelo's passes would not figure in Notre Dame's attack.

Juzwik turned to Angelo and grinned. "Why don't you stay in here where it's warm and curl up with a good book?" Steve suggested. "You won't be worth a nickel to us in that muck."

It is doubtful, though, whether ribbing really affected Angelo's football outlook. Joe Petritz, Notre Dame's sports publicist, called Angelo the calmest player before, during, and after a game since Frank Carideo quarterbacked the 1930 Notre Dame team. Petritz told this anecdote:

Bertelli pitched his best game of the year against a great Navy team, completing 12 out of 18 attempts for 232 yards. He threw a 20-yard touchdown pass to Juzwik; completed two passes to the Navy 8- and 2-yard lines, respectively, to set up Notre Dame's two other touchdowns in the 20 to 18 victory.

"What do you think about when you drop back to pass?" a sports writer asked Angelo, in the locker room, later.

Angelo hitched a towel around his middle, and thought for a moment. "Not much of anything," he finally replied. "You see, I know who the receiver is and where he should be before the play starts. Nine times out of ten, he's there. Then it's automatic. I throw the ball."

His technique was very effective. As a tailback in 1941, he threw for 1,027 yards, with a completion average of .569 that led the nation. But that was not quite good enough for Frank Leahy.

One afternoon, Leahy called Angelo into his office. "Bert," Leahy said, "you are the finest passer and the worst runner I've ever coached. We've got to do something about it."

Leahy diagrammed a Notre Dame pass play on his memorandum pad. "We were lucky last year, Bert. We didn't have any deception. Everybody knew when you were going to pass. You just took the ball from center, dropped back a few yards and threw. No deception, but they'll be laying for us next fall. Think you can play quarterback?"

"I guess so," Angelo replied. "Why?"

Leahy sketched a new offensive diagram. "Because here's what we're going to try out in spring practice. It's the T formation. That means we'll have to discard the Rockne shift, and we may get a few howls from the synthetic alumni, but we're really not throwing Rock's stuff out the window. Rock was using the T formation way back in 1920, long before the Chicago Bears made it popular again."

Leahy drew a big circle on the pad. "This is you, Bert. You'll play right behind center and handle the ball on every play. You'll feed it to the other backs, or you'll fake and drop back to pass—that's where we'll get the deception we lacked last fall. Of course, it means a lot of work for you. You'll have to memorize 50 or 60 new plays next month."

"Sounds good to me," Angelo said. "I think I'll like this T formation."

And like it he did. In 1942, his junior year, he threw for 1,039 yards and ten touchdowns. The following year he won the Heisman Trophy despite the fact that he played in only six games before entering the Marine Corps.

In his 26-game college career at Notre Dame, Bertelli was considered a ball-handling wizard, completing 167 of 318 passes for 2,578 yards and 28 touchdowns. His expertise with the ball was the key reason why legendary coach Frank Leahy decided to scrap the single wing that was in vogue at the time for the T formation in 1942.

Bertelli served in Iwo Jima and Guam, attaining the rank of captain in the Marine Corps. After World War II, Bertelli played professionally in the All-America Football Conference with the Los Angeles Dons in 1946 and the Chicago Rockets in 1946 and 1947

Bertelli

before a severe knee injury ended his career.

Bertelli, who was elected to the National Football Foundation Hall of Fame in 1972, was the third oldest living Heisman winner behind Jay Berwanger and Larry Kelley, the first two Heisman winners, before his death at age seventy-eight, on June 26, 1999.

"The Downtown Athletic club [which awards the Heisman Trophy] and the Heisman family have lost a true friend," said Ruby Riska, the Executive Director of the Heisman Memorial Trust. "Angelo always conducted himself as a class person, never demanding, always giving."

Courtesy of the United States Naval Academy

Bellino

"The older you get, the more the recipient appreciates something like the Heisman Trophy," Joe Bellino told the *Washington Post*'s Bob Fachet, in 1976, "It seems to get more and more important. The press has really caught on to publicizing it . . . "

In 1960, Bellino was the first Naval Academy football player to win the Heisman Trophy. As the nation's best football player, Bellino wound up a collegiate career that in three years had him score 31 touchdowns; rush for 1,664 yards on 330 carries; return 38 kicks for 833 more yards and altogether set thirteen Naval Academy football records.

Bellino's feats pale when compared to today's running backs, but he played both offense and

defense, those being the days of one platoon ball. In fact, his interception in the end zone preserved Navy's 17–12 win over Army in 1960.

Bellino reflected on his days at the Naval Academy from his home in Massachusetts, "It was the perfect place for me to go to school with my abilities and with what I wanted in academics," he said. "If I had to do it again, I would select the Naval Academy.

"I didn't know what lay ahead of me as far as football accomplishments," he continued. "I'm not sure I would have reached those at some place other than Navy. With the ability I had and the type of talent at Navy at the time, I was at the right school . . . the daily routine and healthy environment helped me be a better athlete."

Bellino is quick to stifle any talk that the four-year commitment he fulfilled after graduating from the Naval Academy ruined his chances to play professional football, even though the American Football League (and its attractive bonuses) was just one-year old at the time of his graduation.

"I have no regrets whatsoever," Bellino told a Washington reporter. "I had the opportunity to leave the Academy as a junior and sign a hefty baseball contract, almost six figures, which was a lot of money in 1959. Who knows what would have happened?

"I only know what's happened since. The best four years of my life were in the service. I had the opportunity to live in Japan with my wife and daughter and I traveled all over the world with the Navy."

Bellino did have a brief three-year period with the Boston Patriots, but carefully notes, "Professional football didn't influence my decision to leave the service."

Bellino, often compared to the Maryland blue crab for his abilities to move sideways so quickly, had to run inside, and he used a change of pace rather than sheer speed to dance his way to additional yardage.

Bellino was an outstanding catcher and outfielder on Navy baseball teams. He hit .428 in twenty-two games in 1959 and led the Eastern Intercollegiate League in stolen bases. He had a .320 average in 1960 and was the baseball captain in 1961.

Army partisans can hardly forget the 1959-60 academic year for what Bellino did to the Cadets. In addition to his three-touchdown performance in the 1959 Army-Navy football game, he had an equally sensational day in the Army-Navy baseball game of June Week, 1960. The Cadets had won the Eastern League title and their pitcher had won nine games in a row. Bellino went 4 for 4 at the plate, drove in three runs, stole two bases and threw out two Army runners attempting to steal as the Midshipmen carved out a 9-1 win.

In addition to being a unanimous choice as an All-American in 1960, Bellino won the Maxwell Trophy and capped off his senior year at the Academy by winning the school's top two athletic awards—the Naval Academy Athletic Association Sword and the Thompson Trophy Cup. It was the first time in forty-two years that one midshipman had received both of these awards in the same year.

Bellino's number 27 jersey was retired after the 1960 season. And the man who made the jersey famous, the "player who was never caught from behind," the Winchester Rifle, was selected to the National Football Foundation Hall of Fame in 1977, the tenth Naval Academy player to be selected to the Hall of Fame.

Courtesy of University Photo/Graphics, Pennsylvania State University

J. Cappelletti

John Cappelletti became Penn State's first Heisman Trophy winner in 1973 and went on to become the most honored player in the school's football history.

In addition to the Heisman honor, Cappelletti was named to every All-American team. He was also named winner of the Maxwell Trophy and Player of the Year by the Walter Camp Foundation, the *Football News*, United Press International, the Washington Touchdown Club, and several other organizations.

Cappelletti was also named the "Amateur Athlete of the Year" by the Philadelphia Sports Writers Association and was honored by clubs throughout the country.

The 215-pound Cappelletti from Upper Darby, Pennsylvania, earned that recognition by becoming the first back in Penn State history to rush for more then 1,000 yards two seasons in a row. He had 1,117 yards as a junior and 1,522 yards as a senior.

"Cappy was the best player I've ever been around," said Penn State coach Joe Paterno. "He had speed, power, balance, determination. You knew when you were in a tough game, he'd do something to win it for you."

Penn State lost only one game in which Cappelletti played as a running back, a 28-21 loss to Tennessee in his first start. After that loss, he played in twenty-one consecutive wins for the Lions. He missed the team's 14-0 loss to Oklahoma in the Sugar Bowl when he came down with a flu virus on the day of the game.

The Lion co-captain averaged 5.3 yards per carry in his senior year, gaining 1,522 yards on 286 attempts, and scoring 17 touchdowns. Cappy appeared for only three plays against Syracuse and did not carry the ball because of an injured shoulder. Not including that brief appearance, he averaged 152.2 yards per game rushing. His career totals are 519 carries, 2,639 yards and 29 touchdowns.

The Upper Darby, Pennsylvania native is modest and unassuming and took all of the honors and attention in stride.

"There are many great players in the country," he said after he won the Heisman. "I feel fortunate that so many people have singled me out for recognition."

His acceptance speech at the award ceremony was both gracious and touching. Like so many honorees he thanked his coaches and his family. But he had some very special words for his college coach and special words for his brother, Joseph.

"It was a hard decision making a choice of colleges. At the time, I didn't know that much about it, but I think one thing that swayed me was the man sitting to my right, and that is Coach Paterno. When I was being recruited, he came down to my house, I think he was not only on a recruiting trip, but he was looking for a good meal, an Italian meal. When he came in the door, he looked over and on the couch was my brother Joseph lying there. He was very ill at the time, more so than usual, and Coach Paterno was more concerned and talked more about what he could do for my brother than what he could do to get me to Penn State. For this I am very thankful and I'm glad I had the chance to show some appreciation to this man in the past four years.

"I think everybody here knows mostly about his coaching accomplishments at Penn State. I don't think there is a more dedicated man anywhere concerned with young people and a better teacher of life on and off the field," Cappelletti said.

And then he returned to the subject of his brother.

"The youngest member of my family, Joseph, is very ill. He has Leukemia. If I can dedicate this trophy to him tonight and give him a couple days of happiness, this is worth everything. I think a lot of people think that I go through a lot on Saturdays and during the week as most athletes do, and you get your bumps and bruises and it is a terrific battle out there on the field. Only for me it is on Saturdays and it's only in the fall. For Joseph, it is all year round and it is a battle that is unending with him and he puts up

with much more than I'll ever put up with, and I think that this trophy is more his than mine because he has been a great inspiration to me."

Joey died of Leukemia in 1976. A movie called "Something for Joey" portrays the relationship of the two brothers.

In 1974, John signed with the Los Angeles Rams (first round draft choice) and spent two years grinding out short yardage. In 1976, he was promoted to starting duties and rushed for 688 yards in 177 carries. Placed on the Injured Reserve list in 1979, he was traded to the San Diego Chargers in 1980 and retired after the 1983 season.

Cappelletti was elected to the National Italian American Sports Hall of Fame in 1989.

Courtesy of the New York Jets Public Relations Dept.

V inny Testeverde, winner of the 1986 Heisman Trophy, was born in South Brooklyn, New York, in 1962, son of Al and Josephine Testeverde.

Big Al Testeverde worked as a construction worker. One day while working on a building next to the Downtown Athletic Club in New York and while he was taking a break, Big Al noticed that the Downtown Athletic Club was the home of the Heisman Trophy. He also noticed the pictures of the winners of the trophy hanging on a wall. He pointed to one of his workers, and then pointed at the pictures and made a bold prediction: "Some day my son Vinny's picture will be hanging on that wall along with those other winners."

Testeverde

Big Al's boast turned into reality in 1986 when son Vinny climaxed a brilliant career at the University of Miami by being named winner of the Heisman Trophy.

The year 1986 turned out to be the biggest year of Vinny's short life as he walked away with numerous honors to

Courtesy of the New York Jets Public Relations Dept.

Former New York mayor Rudy Giuliani shakes hands with Testeverde.

go along with the Heisman Trophy, among them: Consensus All-American selection, the Davey O'Brien Award as the nation's top college quarterback, Maxwell Award, Walter Camp Player of the Year Award, Florida Amateur Athlete of the Year, and Italian-American Athlete of the Year.

Testeverde's senior season at Miami was one of the best ever turned in by a college quarterback and his career stats were just as impressive. When he completed his football playing days at Miami, Vinny was the school's all-time leader in passing with 6,058 yards and touchdown passes with forty-eight. He led the NCAA in passer rating as a senior with a 165.8 mark, leading the Hurricanes to an 11-0 record. In his two years as a starter, Testeverde-led Miami teams compiled a brilliant 21-1 record. Barry Switzer, head football coach of the Oklahoma Sooners, one of the most successful college coaches ever, following a game with Miami when Vinny led the Hurricanes on a big comeback victory over the

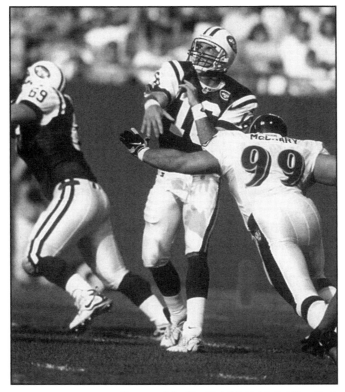

Courtesy of the New York Jets Public Relations Dept.

Testeverde unleashes a bomb.

number one Sooners, said of Testeverde, "In my twenty-one years of coaching, I have never seen a better quarterback than Testeverde."

Vinny's toughest job, though, was getting to Miami. A standout athlete at Elmont High School in New York where he had outstanding stats as a quarterback, Testeverde's trouble wasn't with football but rather with his academic grades. In order to boost his grades, Vinny spent a postgraduate year at Fort Union Military Academy in Virginia where not only did his grades improve but he became bigger and stronger and as he said, "I got smarter as well."

When Testeverde entered Miami on an athletic scholarship, the Hurricanes had two outstanding All-

American quarterbacks on the squad in Jim Kelly and Bernie Kosar. So Big Al's kid waited in the wings knowing that his day would come and making sure he would be prepared by working hard each and every day to improve his skills.

Following his senior season with the Hurricanes, Vinny, who is Miami's leader in career touchdown passes with forty-eight, a mark tied by Steven Walsh, was the number one pick of the Tampa Bay Buccaneers in the NFL draft. Vinny signed with the Bucs in the 1987 season for a then record $8.2 million over six years, two million of which was a signing bonus, an NFL record, at the time, for first-year players.

In 1987, his first season, Vinny earned All-Rookie selection from UPI, *Pro Football Weekly*, and *Football Digest*. In 1989, Vinny twice won NFC Offensive Player of the Week honors and racked up a total of twenty touchdown passes, tying the single-season record set by Doug Williams in 1980.

In 1990, Vinny led the NFC with an average of 7.72 yards per pass attempt. He completed 203 of 365 passes (55.6%) for 2,818 yards with seventeen touchdowns and compiled a career best 75.6 passer rating. He also ran for a career high 280 yards on thirty-eight carries.

Testeverde

Testeverde spent six seasons with the Bucs before moving on to Cleveland in 1993. After three seasons with the Browns, he moved with the team to Baltimore where he played for two seasons, earning his first Pro Bowl honor in 1996. He signed with the New York Jets as a free agent in June of 1998.

Vinny and his wife, Mitzi (a former Bucs cheerleader), have a daughter Alicia Marie and a son Vincent Jr.

U ndisputedly the most decorated player in 1993 was Gino Torretta. The Heisman Trophy winner set eleven school passing marks at the University of Miami, a quarterback factory which has turned out NFL stars Jim Kelly, Bernie Kosar and Vinny Testeverde, as well as, Craig Erickson and Steve Walsh.

Torretta compiled a 26-2 record as a starter for Miami, the most wins ever by a Hurricanes' quarterback, while ranking second in school winning percentage (.928), setting a record for passing yards (7,690), and tossing forty-seven touchdowns, one shy of the school mark of forty-eight held by Testeverde and Walsh. He also set records for total offense with 7,722 yards; single-game passing yards with 485 and

single-game total offense with 474 yards (versus San Diego State in 1991); and longest pass play, a ninety-nine-yard strike to Horace Copeland against Arkansas in 1991. His 123 straight pass attempts without an interception in 1992 smashed the previous record of 116, held by Testeverde and George Mira. His accuracy was among the best in college football.

A unanimous All-American first team selection and Big East Offensive Player of the Year in 1992, Torretta also received the Maxwell

Photo by Rhona Wise

Torretta looks down field for a receiver.

Award, Davey O'Brien Award (given to the top passer in the nation), Johnny Unitas Golden Arm Award and Walter Camp Player of the Year Trophy. He completed 228 of 402 passes (56.7%) for 3,060 yards amid nineteen touchdowns and ranked fifth in the nation, with an average of 276 yards per game.

Torretta put up some phenomenal numbers in 1992, starting with the season opener against Iowa when he completed 31 of 51 passes for 433 yards and a pair of touchdowns in a 24-7 victory to earn ABC-TV Player of the Game honors. He connected on 20 out of 48 passes for 252 yards and two touchdowns, including a game-winning 33-yard toss to Lamar Thomas with 6:50 remaining on the clock to seal the victory over arch rival Florida State. Against

Torretta

West Virginia, Torretta threw for 363 yards on 28 of 40 attempts and three touchdowns in the 35-23 win.

In 1991 Torretta received All-American honorable mention recognition and was named Big East Offensive Player of the Year after passing for 3,095 yards on 205 of 371 attempts with twenty touchdowns and eight interceptions. His 3,155 yards in total offense placed him third on Miami's all-time list. Torretta became only the second Hurricane to throw for over 400 yards (against California in 1990). In 1991 in the season finale against San Diego State, Torretta broke his own school record when he threw for 485 yards on 23 of 44 attempts with touchdowns of 69, 66, 42 and 30 yards in a 39-12 triumph. On January 1, 1992 the national championship was decided in the Orange Bowl, where Torretta led the 'Canes to a 22-0 victory over Nebraska, connecting on 19 of 41 passes for 257 yards and a touchdown.

Torretta played in nine games in 1990 as a backup to Erickson and completed 21 of 41 passes for 210 yards. After Erickson fractured a finger in 1989 against Michigan State, Torretta came off the bench and responded with 15 of 29 completions for 134 yards and a five-yard touchdown pass to Wesley Carroll to give the 'Canes a 26-20 win over the Spartans. He started the next four contests and hit on 101 of 177 passes (57.1%) for 1,325 yards and eight touchdowns. In his first collegiate start, he completed 13 of 16 passes for 239 yards and three touchdowns, including an 88-yarder to Carroll in a 56-0 romp of Cincinnati. He set a school record which he later surpassed when he threw for 468 yards and three touchdowns, completing 32 of 49 passes in a 48-16 win over San Jose State. Torretta did not play in 1988, retaining freshman eligibility.

An All-East Bay, All-Northern California, All-Conference and Academic All-State selection at Pinole Valley High School in California, Torretta established season and career records for completion percentage when he connected on 142 of 240 passes (59.2%) for 1,688 yards and nineteen touchdowns his senior year, adding three scores rushing and another on a pass reception. He also lettered in baseball and track.

A business management major at Miami, the fifth-year senior graduated in 1991 and has begun working on his MBA at Miami. Torretta's brother, Geoff, was a reserve quarterback behind Testeverde at Miami from 1985 to 1986, and also wore number 13. Geoff's twin brother Greg, played wide receiver at Cal-Davis, and the elder brother, Gary, was quarterback at St. Mary's in California. Gino has worked with DARE and the "Join a Team, Not a Gang" campaign in Miami.

Following graduation, Gino was drafted by the Minnesota Vikings. Following one year of service with the Vikings in 1993, he was with the Detroit Lions in 1994 and split the 1995 season between the Lions and the San Francisco 49ers. In the 1996 season, his last in the NFL, he split time between the 49ers and the Seattle Seahawks.

Gino and his wife Bernadette reside in Miami, Florida. Torretta is a financial advisor with Prudential Securities in Miami and covers college football for ESPN.

Courtesy of the University of Wisconsin

Ameche

T
he news was sad that wet August evening in 1988, when word came that Alan "The Horse" Ameche had died in a Houston, Texas hospital of complications following heart bypass surgery.

A native of Kenosha, Wisconsin, Alan Dante Ameche was a four-year starter for Wisconsin (1951–54), and his gridiron exploits during those years were such that they will never be forgotten by Badger enthusiasts.

During those four seasons, Wisconsin teams, coached by Ivan Williamson, won twenty-six games, lost eight and tied three. In sixteen of the games, Ameche ran for over 100 yards, and his running was a key factor in almost every game he played in during his career.

They hung the tag, "The Horse" on Alan in 1951 the first time practice field sideliners saw the big freshman fullback bolt through the tough varsity line (the Badgers of 1951 were the "Hard Rocks" and led the nation in total defense on a yield of 154.8 yards per game) high stepping and sunfishing like a mean rodeo bronco.

Four years later, his style unchanged though bigger, rougher, and tougher, "The Horse" had set a long list of school, Big Ten and NCAA rushing records.

Along the way to All-American honors in 1953 and 1954, and the 1954 Heisman Trophy, Ameche took the Badgers to a share of the 1952 Big Ten title (the first for the school since 1912), and the 1953 Rose Bowl game which the Badgers lost 7-0 to Southern California despite his rushing total of 133 yards on 28 carries. His total included a 54-yard third period romp that set the Badgers up deep in Trojan territory.

Wisconsin's Athletic Publicity Director—they're known as Sports Information Directors nowadays—Art Lentz described Ameche's running style thus: "When he carries the ball, his knees

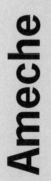

come up high and his arms flail as he roars into the line, yet he can slant like a halfback when it's necessary—witness his effectiveness on pitchouts."

As a freshman, Ameche began breaking Wisconsin rushing records. He amassed 824 yards for an average of 5.2 yards and set a Big Ten mark of 774 in 1952 and was third in 1953. An injury late in the 1954 campaign spoiled his chance to win the third rushing title.

When he had completed his career, he was the NCAA all-time leading rusher at 3,212 yards (not counting his 133 Rose Bowl yards) and he had established a Wisconsin record of twenty-five touchdowns.

Long-time Wisconsin observers likened Ameche to a combination of Pat Harder (1941-1942) and Eddie Jankowski (1935-36), Badger fullbacks of power and elusiveness. UCLA's Red Sanders stated, "Ameche is the strongest runner in football history, not excepting Bronko Nagurski." His own coach, Ivan Williamson, noted, "Alan is a REAL football player."

In 1953, when the rule changes made it necessary to be an all-purpose player, Ameche was a workhorse in the drills and heavy duty chores of defense and offense, which gave him an insight into the requirements of a top-notch fullback.

He learned that a fine ball carrier can create defensive mistakes, and this knowledge served him well. In 1953, his ability to play 55 or more minutes in a game amplified his nickname to "The Iron Horse."

When Alan won the Heisman Trophy in 1954, he was not even aware that he had finished in the top five in his junior year. What the honor meant most to him was a chance to meet his boyhood hero, Doc Blanchard of Army, the 1945 Heisman Trophy winner.

He was drafted by Baltimore, following the 1954 season. In his first professional game against the Chicago Bears at Wrigley Field, he ran 79 yards for a touchdown on his first NFL carry from the line of scrimmage.

In 1955, Ameche led the NFL in rushing and was voted the NFL Rookie of the Year. He was an All-Pro selection from 1955 through 1958 and played in five Pro Bowl games before a severe Achilles tendon injury ended his career after the 1960 season.

Ameche was inducted into the National Football Foundation and College Hall of Fame in 1975. In 1979, he was honored with the NCAA Silver Anniversary Award, which honors those who have led distinguished professional lives after outstanding athletic careers.

In his professional career he ran for 4,045 yards and scored forty touchdowns, but he is most remembered for the one-yard plunge he made against the New York Giants in the 1958 title game to win the game for the Colts 23-17.

Alan once said, "It's probably the shortest run I ever made and the most remembered." John Unitas, the quarterback for the Colts, pointed out, "A lot of people just remember him for that particular run, but he was instrumental in keeping that game alive with his pass catching and running ability."

Unitas was asked why Ameche was given the ball on the game winning play. He responded, "We knew he wouldn't fumble."

Following the end of his professional career, Ameche and former Colts teammate Gino Marchetti went into business together, founding a successful chain of restaurants called "Gino's." Ameche later sold his interest in the restaurants.

Former Wisconsin athletic director Elroy Hirsch remembered Ameche as an individual who never forgot his home town, his home state, or his alma mater. He was unselfish in spite of all his success, and he truly retained his ties to Wisconsin.

Ameche presented his Heisman Trophy to Wisconsin during half-time ceremonies of the 1984 Wisconsin-Northwestern football game in Camp Randall Stadium. He said on that day, "It was the appreciation and the love, I guess you'd say, I have for the school. And I guess that's gotten stronger, too, as the years have worn on."

Gary Messner, Wisconsin's 1954 football team captain, pointed out, "He was the greatest football player I have ever seen. Nobody had to do a great deal of blocking for him. There aren't a lot of guys who could do it all, but he could."

Messner added, "He was a giver, he gave of himself—to friends and charities."

Courtesy of the Pro Football Hall of Fame

Andy Robustelli almost didn't make it to the Pro Football Hall of Fame for the excellent reason that he almost did not play pro football.

In 1951, Andy was drafted in the nineteenth round by the Los Angeles Rams, and the only "bonus" he received was his air transportation to the Rams training camp in California. Even if he stuck with the club, his starting salary was set at only $4,250.

For long hours, Robustelli and his wife Jean weighed the possibility of a pro football career against a high school coaching job which "would offer more security." Even some of his closest friends advised him to take the job in his home state of Connecticut, where he preferred to live.

Once he made the decision to report to the Rams—camp opened on his second wedding anniversary—Robustelli immediately had reason to doubt the wisdom of his choice. He had been considered an outstanding offensive end in college, but with the Rams, he would have to compete with a host of talented veterans, including future Hall of Famers Tom Fears and Elroy (Crazylegs) Hirsch.

How could a raw rookie from a small college beat out these guys?

The answer, of course, was that he couldn't, and Rams coach Joe Stydahar immediately informed him of this.

"If you make it at all," he instructed Robustelli, "it will be as a defensive end, and that is where we are going to give you your shot."

Disappointed, disturbed but realistic—so realistic, in fact, that he didn't even unpack his bags for more than two weeks—Robustelli responded in the only way he knew how—he went all out to make good at what was available to him, the defensive unit.

The first time the Rams held a scrimmage, Robustelli, a bruising 6' 0", 230-pounder, was all over the field. He knocked down ball carriers, smothered passers, and left blockers sprawled on the turf. After the scrimmage he unpacked his bags.

The rest is history, such outstanding history, in fact, that Robustelli was inducted into the Pro Football Hall of Fame in 1971.

Andy was a regular for the championship Los Angeles team in 1951 and the one game he missed that season was the only game he missed in the next fourteen National Football League campaigns. After five great seasons in Los Angeles, Robustelli yearned to play nearer to his home in Stamford, Connecticut, and this yearning finally prompted a trade between the Rams and the Giants. The Rams got a number one draft choice, which turned out to be, incidently, Del Shofner.

Robustelli, happy over his new surroundings, got even better in a Giants uniform. He is credited with molding together the 1956 New York club that won the NFL championship, and he stayed in New York for nine more years, the last three as a player-coach.

Seven times in fourteen years, Andy was named to the All-NFL team as a defensive end. Seven times he performed in the prestigious Pro Bowl. Aside from his Pro Football Hall of Fame election, perhaps his biggest honor came from the Maxwell Club of Philadelphia when that group selected him as the outstanding NFL player in 1962.

Andy, a genuinely modest athlete as well as being a great team leader, was one of the best pass rushing ends the game has ever seen. He did the job with a combination of strength and savvy.

"You've got to know when to rush," Andy explained after he had become a player-coach. "Over-anxiety can hurt you. Knowing when comes with experience, and nothing else."

"There is only one way to play this game," Robustelli said many times, "and that is as hard and as tough as you can."

Long-time Giants coach Allie Sherman agreed and credited this trait as being a major factor in Andy's success.

"Watch Andy on the field," Sherman pointed out, "and you'll be studying a real master. Terrific speed of mind, hands, and feet make him the best. But without his burning desire and his extra determination, he'd be just an average football player."

The fact that Andy was drafted by any pro team at all is somewhat of a miracle. Robustelli played high school football in his native Stamford and, after a Navy hitch, almost matriculated at Villanova. But word from the Villanova coach that he might need a year of brushing up in prep school sent Andy instead to tiny Arnold College, in Millford, Connecticut. (Arnold College is now a part of the University of Bridgeport.)

Andy, who played end and captained the Arnold team for three years, specialized in tackling and blocking kicks, but he was also a very fine pass receiver. Still, Arnold was a small college and the NFL seemed light years away.

The NFL would probably have remained just that—light years away—had it not been for a game at St. Michael's College in Winooski, Vermont, which, ironically, turned out to be the game in which Andy broke a leg, the only serious injury he ever received in football. Rams scout Lou DeFillipo, the ex-Fordham great, was in the stands and saw enough of Robustelli before he got hurt to send a rave notice to Los Angeles.

Even before he completed his playing career, Andrew Richard Robustelli had become a fine businessman and he continues active in a number of successful enterprises. He is playing the business game just like he did the football game—with an extraordinary amount of class!

Robustelli

Courtesy of the Pro Football Hall of Fame

Lavelli

orn February 23, 1923 in Hudson, Ohio, Dante Lavelli played three games as a sophomore at Ohio State in 1942 and then was injured. The next year he was in the United States Infantry, and during his three-and-a-half-year tour of duty, he played no football at all.

Upon his discharge from the Army, Dante elected to pass up his final two years of college eligibility and give professional football a shot. He found a willing taker in his old college coach, Paul Brown, who was just organizing the Cleveland Browns in the new All-America Football Conference. Lavelli signed a Browns' contract early in 1945.

When he reported to training camp that summer,

he was unheralded and by far the least experienced of five players vying for the right end job on the new team.

One candidate was a tested professional. Two were former college stars who had earned national reputations as members of outstanding service teams. The fourth was John Yonaker, a "can't-miss" 6' 4", 225-pounder from Notre Dame.

Yet after the summer skirmishing was over, the first three had been chased out of camp, and Yonaker had been switched to defensive end. That left the 6' 0", 199-pound Lavelli, the guy who had played only three college games, as the Browns' first string right-side receiver.

It was the first great pro triumph for Lavelli and the start of a career that was so sensational that it would bring him pro football's highest honor, induction into the Pro Football Hall of Fame.

Along with Roosevelt Brown, George Connor and Lenny Moore, Dante was enshrined in impressive rites on the front steps of the Hall on August 2, 1975. Immediately following the induction ceremonies, the Washington Redskins squared off in the annual AFC-NFC Hall of Fame game against the Cincinnati Bengals, coached by Paul Brown, the same man who tutored Lavelli first at Ohio State and then throughout his professional career.

It is particularly appropriate that Brown was on the scene because it was his decision when Dante was an Ohio State freshman that may have vaulted Lavelli into all-time greatness.

In high school, Lavelli, the son of an Italian immigrant who came to this country in 1905, had been a standout quarterback and his running and passing had paced the Hudson Explorers to three straight undefeated seasons. He reported to the Buckeyes as a halfback, but Brown soon noticed a flaw in his running style and decided that Dante would be more likely to succeed as an end.

Once he heard of his coach's plans, Lavelli went right to work perfecting his cuts and fakes. By the start of his sophomore season, he had the starting end job hooked up. Three games into the season against Southern California, he was injured and did not play again in the college ranks.

On his discharge from the Army, Lavelli first thought of turning to professional baseball. While in high school, he had been offered a contract with the Detroit Tigers farm system.

Dante opted instead for a professional football career.

"I had seen a pro game in New York. One of my Ohio State buddies was playing for the Giants," Lavelli explained. "I thought if he could make the grade, so could I. So when Brown, my old coach, offered me a chance, I was really ready."

Brown never was sorry that he placed his confidence in Lavelli, for Dante was a star right from the first game. He led the AAFC in receptions as a rookie with 40 catches for 843 yards, a scintillating 21.8-yard average per catch, and eight touchdowns. He capped a brilliant season, in which he was also named to the official All-AAFC team, by catching the winning touchdown pass in the championship game against the New York Yanks.

As a pro "sophomore," Dante upped his catch total to forty-nine and once again won All-AAFC against the Los Angeles Dons. That's the way it was for "Glue Fingers" throughout the four years that the powerful Browns were tearing up the AAFC.

Once the inter-league war ended and the Browns entered the National Football League, skeptics were loudly questioning how well the Cleveland team and its many supposed stars would fare in the so-called "faster company" of the NFL.

The Browns as a team responded to the challenge as did all of the team's leading individuals. Lavelli was no exception. He caught thirty-seven passes his first year in the NFL and, in the famous 1950 championship game between the Browns and the Los Angeles Rams, the team that had deserted Cleveland in 1946, Dante caught eleven passes and scored two touchdowns as the Browns won, 30-28.

The sleek receiver earned All-NFL acclaim in 1951

Lavelli

and 1953 and won starter's roles in three of the first five Pro Bowl games. Without a doubt, he was one of the most vital cogs in the awesome Cleveland machine that brought the Browns six divisional and three NFL championships in their first six years in the league.

Through the years, Lavelli became the favorite target of Otto Graham, Cleveland's super passer and field general. For his eleven-year career, Lavelli wound up with 386 receptions for 6,488 yards and sixty-two touchdowns. All but twenty of his receptions came while Graham was triggering the attack.

Like any great pass-catch team, Graham and Lavelli spent long hours learning the other's every habit.

Dante was a dedicated pattern-runner but once there was a hint that things weren't going right, he preferred to take off down the field and then look back toward Graham and yell for the ball.

"That hollering helped me more than once," Graham, also a Hall of Famer, admits. "Dante had a voice that seemed to penetrate and it was a welcome sound when a couple of big tackles were bearing down on me. We hit more than once for touchdowns on one of those broken plays."

Another favorite Lavelli play was a trick he had copied from Don Hutson, the fabled ace of the Green Bay Packers. Dante would race

for the goal posts, swing around a post with one hand and then be ready to grab a perfectly-thrown pass from Graham when he appeared on the other side.

Lavelli is remembered as quick and sneaky fast but not exceptionally fast. He worked hard on his patterns but he was much more ready to abandon his route in case of trouble than the classic pattern-runner of the Raymond Berry type.

"I think Dante has the strongest hands I've ever seen," Brown once observed. "When he goes up for a pass and a defender goes up with him, you can be sure Lavelli will have the ball when they come down. Nobody can ever take it away from him once he gets his hands on it."

Graham seconded his coach's praise. "We had a lot

of great receivers on the Browns but, when it came to great hands, there was nobody like Old Spumoni. There was no better competitor, either," he said.

Graham retired after the 1955 championship game but Lavelli was persuaded to stay for one more year. "Glue Fingers" was still one of the Browns' leading receivers but catching passes from a new corps of quarterbacks just wasn't the same. So he called it quits at the age of thirty-three.

Both as an individual and as a member of a team that had made winning championships a way of life, Dante had experienced about everything good there was to enjoy in professional football. The only thing left was that coveted spot in the Pro Football Hall of Fame that became a reality in 1975.

Dante Lavelli truly made it all the way from absolute bottom to absolute top in the pro football world.

He was elected to the National Italian American Sports Hall of Fame in 1981.

Courtesy of the Pro Football Hall of Fame

Marchetti

Ernest and Maria Marchetti always had the somewhat normal parental fear that their son, Gino, would be hurt playing football.

"Whatever you do, Gino," the elder Marchetti used to say, "stay out of the other boys' way, so they don't hurt you."

Every quarterback who played in the National Football League in the 1950s and early 1960s fervently wished that Gino had followed his father's advice.

But Gino Marchetti, 6' 4", 245 pounds and extremely talented, did not listen to his father. Instead, he wound up as "the greatest defensive end in pro football history," as selected by a special panel of experts in 1969. Many will say that a better pass rusher never lived.

So it could be expected that at the first moment he was eligible after a mandatory five-year retirement period, Gino Marchetti was tapped for membership in the Pro Football Hall of Fame. Pro football's highest honor became official for Gino on July 29, 1972 when he, Lamar Hunt, Ollie Matson, and Ace Parker were inducted in impressive ceremonies on the front steps of the Hall of Fame in Canton.

It is an irony that Ernest Marchetti, who had shunned opportunities to see his son play in high school, college and the early years of pro football, finally did tune in on the national telecast of the 1958 NFL championship game between Gino's team, the Baltimore Colts, and the New York Giants.

The game turned out to be "the greatest game ever played." The Colts won in overtime, 23-17. Gino, however, wasn't around at the finish. He had suffered a severely broken ankle late in the fourth period while making a critical tackle of the Giants' Frank Gifford. Marchetti's teammate, 300-pound Gene (Big Daddy) Lipscomb, fell on top of Gino after the tackle to cause the injury.

Marchetti's stop proved to be a key play, for it ended the Giants' drive and gave Baltimore the ball. From there, the Colts went on to tie the game in the final seconds of regulation play and then to win it in overtime. Gino stayed on the sidelines until the game was tied but was taken to the locker room in the overtime period.

"The docs were afraid the crowd might trample me if we scored," Gino explained. "I was stretched out on the table when I heard the guys coming in. I could tell they won, they were all whooping it up. Right then, that ankle stopped hurting!"

Many felt that the injury would prematurely end Marchetti's brilliant career. As it turned out, all it did was prevent him from setting an all-time record for Pro Bowl appearances.

The record book shows that Gino played in ten Pro Bowl games in an eleven-year stretch from 1955 to 1965 and missed only the 1959 game. He had already been chosen to play in the game when he suffered his injury. During the same period, Gino was All–NFL seven times, missing only 1963 in the 1957 to 1964 span.

Even in his final full season in 1964, Marchetti continued to perform with the same enthusiasm that had characterized his play throughout his NFL career.

Gino was an all-around brilliant defender, but he was best known for his vicious pass rushing techniques. Marchetti was known for clean, but hard play and was a particular terror on third down in an obvious passing situation. When opponents double-teamed, and sometimes triple-teamed him, that only served to make the rest of the Colts' rush more effective.

Marchetti was also adept at stopping the running play. He could recover quickly to close the inside holes and he could swing wide to stymie end sweeps. He was the Colts' captain through much of his career, and he was highly respected by his teammates and a tremendous favorite with Baltimore's rabid fandom.

All of this was a remarkable accomplishment for the product of an Italian immigrant family who never really showed much football talent until he was a high school senior. A year after his graduation, at seventeen, he was serving in the United States Army and fighting in the pivotal Battle of the Bulge.

After the war, he organized the Antioch Hornets, a semi–pro town team, and this was important to the Marchetti story in that he attracted the attention of a scout from Modesto Junior College. After a year at Modesto, Gino was sought out by the University of San Francisco whose coach, Joe Kuharich, was building the foundations of a football powerhouse.

At USF, Marchetti developed into the finest tackle on the West Coast, winning All-Coast and All-Catholic honors in his senior season in 1951. One of his USF teammates, halfback Ollie Matson joined Marchetti as a fellow 1972 enshrinee into the Pro Football Hall of Fame.

Gino's pro career started discouragingly because

of the unique team situation that developed right after Marchetti's second round selection by the New York Yanks in the 1952 draft. The Yanks franchise moved to Dallas for the 1952 season. Then the hapless Texans folded after one year, and Marchetti's contract was assigned to Baltimore, which was setting up shop again after the original Colts had folded after the 1950 season.

The new Colts were a second-division team but, as they built toward championship status, so too did Marchetti develop into super-star proportions. He played in his first Pro Bowl after his first season in Baltimore. Marchetti was always determined to retire before he lost his great effectiveness, and he tried to quit after the 1963 season, when he had also served as a defensive line coach for the Colts. But the Colts had high championship hopes in 1964 and they coaxed Gino out of retirement. After the 1964 campaign, he retired again.

Almost two years later, in November 1966, he was asked to play again when the Colts, in title contention, suffered heavy injuries on their defensive line. So Gino came back. He played only four games and, for the only time in the 161 times he answered the gun in the NFL, he wasn't super-effective. In one way, coming out of retirement was a mistake. In another way, it showed just what kind of guy Gino was—and is.

"As far as I am concerned, I am not making a comeback," Gino explained. "I'm doing them a favor. Everything I have I owe to them and if they think I can help, I have to give it a try."

Gino was referring to more than the obvious advantages pro football had provided. He was mindful of the help Colts' owner Caroll Rosenbloom had given him midway in his career when he insisted that Gino start in some type of business and then loaned him the cash to get started.

Gino and his associates started a chain of quick-order restaurants which grew to more than 300. Now a millionaire, Gino also owns a highly successful restaurant in Wayne, Pennsylvania.

Marchetti

Unlike many great athletes who can never quite let go, Gino has been content to concentrate on his business and more or less stay away from the game to which he contributed so greatly. But of course, that's not totally possible.

People in the little town of Lucca, Italy, may or may not be aware that there is such a thing as the Pro Football Hall of Fame.

But this far-away place is important to the pro grid shrine for it has produced two members of the Hall of Fame. In one case, the tie is direct and in the other indirect, but the distinction is unique in any case.

Leo Nomellini, a defensive tackle with the San Francisco 49ers for fourteen years and a member of the 1969 class of the Pro Football Hall of Fame, was born in Lucca in 1924. His parents moved to Chicago while Leo was a baby.

Gino Marchetti, also a fourteen-year NFL veteran, is a member of the 1972 class. His parents, Ernest and Maria had immigrated to America. Their home town? Lucca, Italy!

Marchetti

Courtesy of the Miami Dolphins

D an Marino was born in Pittsburgh, Pennsylvania on September 15, 1962. He was a standout quarterback for Central Catholic High School, winning Parade All-American honors. He also won an offer from the Kansas City Royals to play baseball.

His dad was Marino's official coach at St. Regis, a Catholic school right across the street from his house. Marino became the school's quarterback, but was almost kicked off the team because his grades were so bad. "Danny could recall everything from a bubble-gum card but couldn't remember when the Civil War started," his father told *Sports Illustrated*. After his dad told him he wouldn't be allowed to play football unless he studied harder, Marino hit

Marino

the books. He brought his grades up just enough to be accepted to Central High School, one of the best schools for athletics in the city.

Marino was a multi-sport star in high school, playing both baseball and football. A pitcher in baseball, he earned a 25-1 record during his career and threw the ball as fast as 92 miles-per-hour.

He also batted .550 in his senior year. But, it was on the football field, however, that Marino received the most attention, playing quarterback as well as punting and place kicking.

He grew up very close to Pitt Stadium, where he would build a career with the University of Pittsburgh Panthers. Part way through his freshman year he became the starting quarterback. The next three years the Panthers won thirty-one times with only one loss and went to the Fiesta, Gator, and Sugar Bowls. His best year was his junior year, completing 226 of 380 passes, thirty-seven of them for touchdowns.

Partly because he threw more interceptions than touchdowns in his disappointing senior season at Pitt, he was not drafted by the NFL teams until the twenty-seventh round. Miami Dolphins coach Don Shula could not believe he was still available, but he was extremely happy.

Early in the 1983 season, Marino became the starting quarterback for the Dolphins—a surprising accomplishment for a rookie. He led the Dolphins to the American Football Conference (AFC) Eastern Division title that year and was named the NFL's Rookie of the Year. He was also a starting quarterback in the Pro Bowl.

In 1984 Marino became the first quarterback to pass for more than 5,000 yards in a single season, and he broke the single-season record for touchdown passes, with forty-eight. He was voted NFL Player of the Year, and in the postseason he led the Dolphins to the 1985 Super Bowl which they lost to the San Francisco 49ers. In subsequent years, Marino became famous for his throwing power and accuracy. He quarterbacked the Dolphins to numerous playoff appearances.

Marino holds twenty-four NFL records, including the all-time record for pass attempts, completions, yardage, and touchdown passes, and shares seven more. Showing his durability and consistency, he took the fewest games ever to record 100 touchdowns (45), 200 touchdowns (89), and 300 touchdowns (138).

Marino's final stats reflect why he is considered the greatest passing quarterback of all time. Marino played seventeen years, all with the Dolphins. He appeared in 242 games, starting 240.

He set NFL records in passing attempts (8,358), completions (4,867), yards (61,361), and touchdowns (420).

"I can't think of any athlete who is more identifiable with his team and his community," said Dolphins owner Wayne Huizenga, who at Marino's retirement press conference, announced that the team was retiring the quarterback's number 13 jersey, building a statue of him outside the stadium, and naming a street for him.

Despite those honors, Huizenga and the Dolphins were not interested in having Marino back for the 2000 season. But they did not want the most popular player in Dolphins history to finish his career with a different team, either.

With Jimmy Johnson's retirement, Marino had hoped that new coach Dave Wannstedt would encourage him to stick around. But that encouragement never came, partly because Wannstedt's main allegiance was to his former boss, Johnson, with whom Marino had feuded.

Marino joined HBO Sports as a commentator on "Inside the NFL" in 2000. Marino is also very active in community service and in 1992, started the Dan Marino Foundation that helps support many South Florida Charities.

He will be inducted in the National Football Foundation and College Hall of Fame in 2003.

Marino

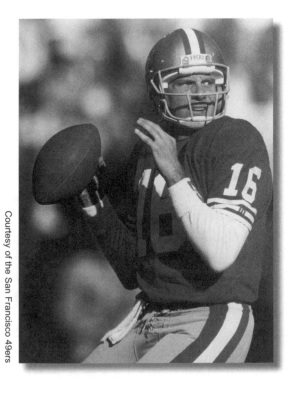

Courtesy of the San Francisco 49ers

Joe Montana was born June 11, 1956, in New Eagle, Pennsylvania and raised in Monongahela, Pennsylvania. He was the only child of Joe Sr. and Theresa Montana. Joe played many sports, including baseball, football, and basketball. He was on the Pennsylvania State Runner-up Basketball Team in 1973, and was offered a scholarship at North Carolina Sate, which was National Champion in 1947.

But football was his first choice. He was the starting quarterback for his high school team for two years, was named a Parade All-American his senior year, and accepted the offer to play for Notre Dame. His sophomore year at Notre Dame got him a reputation as a come from behind quarterback, as he entered games with his team trailing and rallied the team for a win. (In his NFL years, the Comeback Kid would lead 31 fourth-quarter comebacks.) However, he did not become the starter until his junior year when, in the third game of the season, he rallied the team again. They finished that year as National Champions. He continued to lead the Irish his senior year to a good year, but no championship.

Of the countless fabled names in Notre Dame's football past, the one that still prompts as many questions as any other, in the Notre Dame sports information department is that of Joe Montana, quarterback of Notre Dame's 1977 National Championship team. Many visitors to Note Dame's Heritage Hall often are surprised to discover that Montana never received All-American status and was not selected until the third round of the National Football League draft. Interest in Montana's exploits remains keen partly because of his stardom in the NFL and partly because his five years at Notre Dame were so eventful.

Joe Montana, a third-round draft choice of the San Francisco 49ers, was not a very impressive team at the time. By the end of his second season he became their starting quarterback as the team made a dramatic improvement. In 1981, their first winning season in some time, Montana led them to the Super Bowl Championship. The next championship season would come in 1984, when Montana had a great year. He passed for more than 3,600 yards, and had a quarterback rating of 102.9—the best in the conference. It was so good that he was overshadowed only by fellow Pennsylvanian Dan Marino of the Miami Dolphins. The teams seemed destined to meet in the Super Bowl, and they did, battling head to head, and Montana had the better day as the 49ers won, 38-16.

Montana was a master of late-game comebacks. He directed his team to 31 fourth-quarter come-from-behind wins during his career, including a 92-yard drive in the closing seconds of Super Bowl

XXIII. His uncanny ability to bring a team back from apparent defeat was so common that it simply became referred to as "Montana Magic."

A true student of the game, Montana won the NFL passing title in both 1987 and 1989. He topped the NFC in passing five times: 1981, 1984, 1985, 1987, and 1989. Thirty-nine times he passed for more than 300 yards in a game, including seven times in which he surpassed 400 yards. His six 300-yard passing performances in the postseason are an NFL record. He also owns the career playoff record for attempts, completions, touchdowns, and yards gained in passing.

Montana led his team to the playoffs eleven times. Along the way, he captured nine divisional championships and victories in four Super Bowls, of which he was chosen as the MVP three times.

Named All-NFL three times and All-NFC on five occasions, Montana was voted to the Pro Bowl eight times, which was a league record for a quarterback at the time.

In 1992 after missing 31 consecutive games due to an injury to his throwing arm, Montana made a dramatic comeback. In the second half of the regular season finale, a Monday Night Football game versus the Detriot Lions, Montana performed his magic of old—completing 15 of 21 passes for 126 yards and two touchdowns as the 49ers defeated the Lions 24-6.

In 1993 Montana joined the Kansas City Chiefs to finish out his career. He took another mediocre team and helped turn it around. Although there would be no Super Bowls, the team was very successful while Montana was there. In 1993, injuries again took their toll. Another ruptured disk limited Montana to eleven starts, but Kansas City won the division championship and two playoff games. In the AFC title game, a concussion knocked Montana out of the game in the third quarter, and the Chiefs lost the game.

Montana

The next year would be Joe's last. Although posting only a 9–7 record, the Chiefs did make it into the playoffs, but lost in the first round.

Joe Montana showed his abilities, not only as quarterback, but as a leader. He was able to rally the other players on two NFL teams and, with his leadership, turn them from below average teams to excellent ones. He was a first-ballot inductee into the Pro Football Hall of Fame and was enshrined in July of 2000. He was elected to the National Italian American Sports Hall of Fame in 1996–1997.

Courtesy of the New England Patriots

G. Cappelletti

Gino Cappelletti was one of the greatest players in Boston Patriots and American Football League history.

Gino was born on March 26, 1934 in Keewatin, Minnesota, and played at the University of Minnesota. Signed as a free agent defensive back off a Minneapolis sandlot in 1960, Gino switched to wide receiver the following season. In addition to playing wide receiver, he handled the Patriots' place kicking chores and in the process set a host of club and AFL records. He still ranks as the Patriots' all-time leading scorer with 1,130 points (176 field goals, 350 PATs, and 42 touchdowns) and was the AFL scoring leader five times. A five-time AFL All-Star, he was one of only three players to play in all of his team's games during the AFL's existence. Only offensive tackle Tom Neville (159 games) played more games as a Patriot than Gino, who appeared in 153 games before retiring prior to the start of the 1971 season. During his career, he caught 292 passes for 4,574 yards.

Cappelletti joined the Patriots as a special teams coach in May of 1979. In his first two seasons as special teams coach, Gino instructed All-Pro kicker John Smith into becoming the NFL's most accurate career field goal kicker. Under Cappelletti's guidance, Smith won back-to-back NFL scoring titles in 1979 and 1980.

Prior to joining the Patriots staff, Gino served as the color commentator on the Patriots radio broadcasts for seven seasons and pursued a career in the restaurant and food service industry.

Saluted as one of only three men to play every game in the ten-year history of the AFL, "Duke" was the AFL's all-time scoring king. On November 10, 1968, he became the first man in league history to score more than 1,000 career points. He smashed the magic barrier with the reception of a touchdown pass in the rain against San Diego. He won league scoring titles five times (1961, 1963-1966), only Don Hutson of the Green Bay Packers (1940-1944) won as many titles. In addition to fame as a point maker with his toe, Gino excelled as a pass receiver. He had 250 receptions, 4,000 yards and 40 touchdowns. A five-time AFL All-Star, he holds the league scoring record (1964) with 155 points. Cappelletti also set league records with six field goals in one game (1964 against Denver) and 28 points in one game (1965 against Houston).

For more than two decades, Gino has provided the analysis on the radio broadcast of all Patriots games with Gil Santos as the play-by-play announcer. He was inducted into the National Italian American Sports Hall of Fame in 1984.

G. Cappelletti

HOCKEY

P hil Esposito opened the door to hockey for Italian Americans and went on to become the greatest center in National Hockey League history.

Esposito was a star in the NHL for eighteen years, playing with the Chicago Black Hawks, the Boston Bruins, and the New York Rangers.

Phil's list of accomplishments and records could probably take the length of the Boston Garden ice to display. In a career that ended during the 1980-1981 season, Esposito racked up a total of 717 goals and 873 assists for 1,590 points.

A year before Esposito retired, another Italian American was making ice hockey history.

On February 22, 1980, at Lake Placid, New York, the United States Olympic Hockey team stunned the hockey world by winning the gold. The USA was captained by Mike Eruzione, who scored the winning goal in a 4-3 victory over the heavily favored USSR. The USA then went on to defeat Finland for the Gold Medal.

Both Esposito and Eruzione are members of the National Italian American Sports Hall of Fame.

Courtesy of Boston University

There isn't a day that goes by when someone doesn't walk up to Mike Eruzione to tell him where they were when the USA Olympic Hockey Team upset the USSR, 4-3, a historic victory for the USA.

Eruzione knows where he was that historic night. He was on the ice at Lake Placid, New York, scoring the game-winning goal.

Two days later, the Americans and Eruzione shocked the hockey world once again by defeating Finland, 4-3, to capture the gold.

"It was great to be part of a great victory for the USA," Eruzione said. "And for my teammates to elect me captain of the team was a great honor and tribute to me."

Eruzione

Courtesy of Boston University

Eruzione heads toward the net.

Eruzione

Eruzione showed his appreciation on the ice by scoring three goals and adding five assists.

A native of Massachusetts, born in Winthrop, on October 25, 1954, Eruzione was an outstanding high school athlete gaining all-scholastic honors in baseball, football, and hockey. He continued his education and athletic heroics at Boston University where he captained the hockey team in his senior year. In his four years at BU, the Terriers won the Eastern Collegiate Championship each year.

Mike captured many individual honors as well. He was named the best defensive forward in the East all four years and was inducted into Boston University Athletic Hall of Fame.

Following graduation from Boston University, Eruzione played two years with the Toledo Gold Diggers in the International Hockey League, but was still allowed to keep his amateur status. Eruzione gained more honors for his hard and skillful work on the ice when he captured the McKenzie Award, which is awarded to the most outstanding American-born hockey player in the International Hockey League each year.

Eruzione was chosen to join the USA Olympic Team in 1981. What he and his teammates accomplished during "The Miracle on Ice" at Lake Placid will long be remembered. Mike was later inducted into the Olympic Hall of Fame.

Even President Jimmy Carter was caught up in "The Miracle on Ice."

"Let them all know how much we love them," said Carter. "Here at the White House we were watching the TV with one eye and working on Iran and the other problems with the other eye."

Eruzione knew deep down that the USA would bounce back after trailing Finland for the first two periods in the gold medal game. "Right from the first shift out there, I didn't think they could skate with us. I knew we could beat them," he said.

Following the clinching game, USA coach Herb Brooks, as he was shaking hands with his captains praised his team for a great effort. "You are watching a group of people who startled the athletic world—not the hockey world, but the athletic world."

The USA Hockey Team, along with other Olympic participants, were honored by President Carter at a White House brunch where they stuffed themselves with roast beef while wearing cowboy hats and carrying tiny American flags. When the Bay State players on the USA team arrived at Logan Airport in Boston, Eruzione was missing his flag. When asked what happened to it, he replied, "Roz [Mrs. Carter] has it."

In recent years, Mike has spent time in New York and New Jersey as a commentator for Madison

Square Garden Communications Network. He has provided coverage of the New York Rangers and New Jersey Devils games and also conducted special interviews with players and coaches.

In preparation for the 1984 Olympics, Mike worked in conjunction with Anheuser-Busch on the Olympic Art Work Project to raise funds for the Los Angeles games. Mike and many other former Olympians raised thousands of dollars for the cause. In 1984, Mike broadcast both the Winter Games from Sarajevo, Yugoslavia and the Summer Games from Los Angeles for ABC Sports.

For the past several years, Mike Eruzione has traveled throughout the United States for major corporations and organizations as a motivational speaker and sports promoter.

Since 1993, Mike has been director of development for athletes and assistant hockey coach at Boston University. "I was looking for something that was a little more Monday through Friday," said Eruzione, who has a wife, Donna, two sons, and a daughter. "Not only do I work on the athletic side of fundraising, but I also help out with the hockey team. So it's kind of given me a little of both worlds."

Eruzione

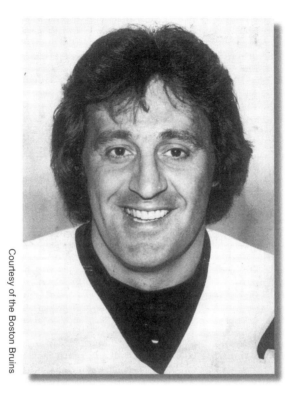

Courtesy of the Boston Bruins

Phil Esposito had four hockey lives. He was a young star with the Chicago Black Hawks with whom he began his illustrious hockey career.

"I spent most of my time on the bench that season. When I did get a chance to play, I was so nervous about making a mistake that I really didn't do as well as I should have," he said.

In 1965, Esposito was switched from checking lines and spot duty and was given a shot on a new line with Bobby Hull and Chico Maki. "Let's face it, Hull had to be the best player in the game," Phil said. Needless to say, the line exploded with goals coming in net-fulls.

One other thing exploded at this time.

Esposito

"Gordie Howe was always my idol," Phil said. "Then to know I'd be skating on the same ice with him gave me goose pimples." However, at Chicago Stadium, Howe nailed Esposito with a bonecrusher when Phil didn't even have the puck. "That hero worship stopped right there!" Phil said.

Esposito had begun his career in the minors at St. Louis in 1962 with 36 goals and 90 points in only 71 games. In 1964 he started off with a rush—80 points in just 43 games and the Black Hawks put in the call to get his body to Chicago pronto.

"The big difference I found between the minors and the NHL is checking," Phil said. "Guys are on you so quickly that you don't have that extra second to make a pass or get a shot away.

"The skating is the same. There were many guys in the Central League who could skate up in the NHL as well as any of them, but they could not check or take one. In the NHL, when you get the puck you fly! If you don't you'll have two guys working you over real good."

Esposito did his homework and paid his dues—he was a great corner digger and there are very few of them. "He was a big, rugged kid," said Chicago Black Hawks general manager Tommy Ivan. "He didn't mind piling into the corner to fight for puck possession. That's a rugged, thankless job, and you usually get only bruises for your effort. You don't get too many good corner diggers because it takes a guy with guts and a strong fighting spirit to do it. Phil was that kind of player."

Ivan's assessment should prove to the boo-birds that Phil Esposito was not a one-way player. The Boston fans, in his second life, saw him hug the net, and patrol the crease in front of the goalie all the time. Phil got a lot of flack for being just a "shooter" and not a full team player.

Hockey fans should realize that Esposito paid his dues in bruises and bumps. He did the digging, the body checking, the line patrolling, the ragging to kill penalties, and the hounding of the other team's stars

Esposito

with forechecking and hacking up and down the lanes.

So he did not begin his career in front of the crease. He earned that spot the hard way. He was a goal scorer, a strange animal in the hockey pecking order. Every hockey player can shoot the puck, but only a special few can find a hole, see a hole opening, or fake the goalie well enough to be able to work the corners or shoot between the goalie's legs.

Courtesy of the Boston Bruins

Phil Esposito hugs the net.

This art, and art it is, was practiced by Esposito like no other until a fellow named Wayne Gretzky came along.

Phil was the essence of the Bruins. Bobby Orr played unparalleled defense, and he was the best scoring defenseman and puck handler and shooter and skater ever combined in a defenseman.

Esposito was the man who muscled his way into the scoring zone and let no one push him out of there. He racked up fantastic goal totals in his time and he even passed off to the Orrs and Cashmans or whoever was open when he was blocked.

General manager Milt Schimidt once said, "You see Phil on the ice and you don't see him. Sure, he's

Esposito

big, but he seems to move slowly, he leans on people and you look to see if anything is really happening and the red light blinks again—Esposito scored another. He's so quick you don't see him do anything."

Phil said in reply, "You can't sit on the puck and see what you are going to do with it. Once you look, it's gone. I don't see a goalie. If you look for him to see what he does, he's already moved and so have his defensemen—right for you."

As quiet as Esposito was on the ice, he was even quieter off the ice. He could laugh and joke with the best and had a grin that split his face in half each time he let it out. But when the pals went home, the party broke up, or the team bus brought them back to the hotel, Phil had on his thinking cap. He always looked beyond where he was.

He saw many of the players with poor educations; they came through the Junior systems where practice was more important than a classroom. Others had high school educations in name only and were looking at their NHL careers as a world that would never end. Phil was a superstar who cared. That alone sets him apart from his peers. The other big money men built high walls around themselves to shield themselves from the problems of their world of hockey and investments.

Esposito

With the Rangers, his third life, Esposito was brought in to shore up a sagging outfit, a team that simply could not win the big ones. He had lost a step or two from his prime but he always could find the open shot. Thus, he scored, but his production was nowhere near his Bruin output. He could see the time clock on the wall ticking off his last gasps for breath after a turn on the ice.

Finally, he could not hack it anymore and he decided to end his career at 38 years of age. And in that year, 1981, he sat for the first time with no train to catch, no plane, no bus, no cab. No club offered to add him to its front office, none wanted him even as a scout—and who could find a scorer or recognize one faster and better than Phil?

He had always confided in his wife, who shared his feelings about the game and life in general.

He had all the money he needed, his family was in fine shape and he had a loving wife.

But what shocked him was the reality of his hockey pension. "When I retired, I couldn't believe what happens to a guy. I had really thought about it and how it would be for the players I knew, but it chilled me when I saw the figures. I looked at the pension and said, 'How the hell can a guy live on that?' I had played for twenty years—imagine other guys who played only a few years, how would they do?"

Of course, Phil had no financial worries, but he felt for the guys who would be faced with that same traumatic bombshell and were unprepared to face it and to weather it. To be successful in a later career, they would need to survive.

Phil said he was spending too much time watching TV soap operas. So he asked his wife what she thought he should be doing.

"She told me! 'You always felt that something should be done for the guys. Why don't you make that a project?' "

So he founded the Phil Esposito Foundation—his fourth life. He had done his share of TV, speaking out against drugs, and talking to school kids about getting their act together. But the Foundation was something different.

It helped ex-players find counseling and proper jobs, and it helped families of deceased players.

That is why Phil is a man of many facets. While active, he won about every honor a player can collect. He set important records for scoring in playoff games and then broke his own records. He set season scoring records and then topped those, too.

A point to remember is that he reached levels considered unreachable. The four-minute mile was a mental as well as physical block. But the Australians trained by running up sand dunes and punctured the pain barrier that daunted all who went before. So by their committed effort, they broke the four-minute mile barrier. Once the barrier was broken, the flood gates opened and many went through.

Esposito broke the 100-point barrier the first time in the 1968–69 season. He "slumped" to ninety-nine in 1969–70, but then topped the century mark in 1970–71 with a fantastic 152 points, including seventy-six goals. And he topped 100 points in five continuous seasons. Orr topped the century mark as a defenseman and the barrier was busted wide open. The flood began and Gretzky, who came after it, knew no barriers. The Great Gretzky needed no help, but he did not face breaking the point barrier as Esposito had.

In the evolution of play, team accomplishments, and personal highs, Phil took over from Bobby Hull, who expanded what Maurice Richard had started. He was a trendsetter, one who carried the torch of performance even higher than the one who passed it on to him.

It is no wonder he now carries loving care to new heights in a new field of hockey-after.

Esposito was elected to the Hockey Hall of Fame in 1984.

Esposito

BASKETBALL

For eleven years, Forrest DeBernardi was a dominant player in the college and the Amateur Athletic Union (AAU) ranks. A two-time All-American at Westminster College in 1920 and 1921, "Red" was granted permission by the faculty to play on the Kansas City Athletic Club (KCAC) basketball team which finished third in the AAU National Tournament in 1920 and won the Tournament in 1921. From 1922 through 1929, DeBernardi was associated with the KCAC team, the Hillyard Chemical Company team, and the Cook Paint Company team. When he retired in 1929, he had participated in ten national AAU tournaments and was named to the AAU All-American team eight times. On five of those occasions, Forrest was a member of a national championship team. To show his dominance in the sport, the Associated Press selected DeBernardi as the center on its all-time all-American college basketball team in 1938.

Courtesy of Stanford University

Angelo (Hank) Luisetti was ahead of his time. The Stanford University basketball wizard of the late 1930s set the tone of present day hoop-la by popularizing the one-hand shot.

Hank further immortalized himself by sinking fifty points against Duquesne in the era of low-scoring games and the over-sized ball, which was later reduced in size to make scoring easier.

That fifty points still stands as a single-game scoring record at Stanford—a record which probably not too many major schools can equal. Scoring fifty points in the current dizzy hardwood game is no small feat, even among the pros. And one must remember that the professional game is forty-eight

Luisetti

minutes in length com-
pared with forty minutes of
the collegiate game.

A native of San Francisco,
Luisetti graduated from
Galilee High School where
he was an All-City selec-
tion for three years, Hank
tossed up his accurate one-
handers with both feet on
the floor. "I often wonder
just how they do it," the
Cardinal legend once said
about the one-hand jump
shot.

Hank and his Stanford
teammates made national
headlines in 1936 at New
York's Madison Square

Courtesy of Stanford University

Luisetti poses for a publicity shot.

Garden where the New York teams were dominating the game.

The proud bearers of the Pacific Coast Conference crown,
Stanford bowled over Temple a few days before at
Philadelphia, 45-38.

Stanford then moved into New York to take on
the famed Long Island University Blackbirds
coached by Clair Bee. LIU had won forty-three
straight with a lineup that included the likes of All-
American Jules Bender and a couple of other aces,
Ben Kramer and Art Hillhouse.

Some 17,263 fans packed Madison Square Garden
to get a peek at the one-hand shooting Luisetti who
was already a sensation. What, the crowd wondered,
could he do it against a topflight club like LIU?

Those New Yorkers got their money's worth. LIU
held the Cards to an 11-11 tie early in the game, but
Stanford and Luisetti moved ahead, 22-14, at the

half. Luisetti scored "only fifteen points" as Stanford went on to win, 45-31, with little difficulty—thanks to Hank. He hit his one-handers from every angle and showed onlookers what a tremendous team player he was—rebounding and passing with great accuracy and stealing the ball time and again from the surprised Blackbirds.

Even after such a victory there were the usual skeptics. Nat Holman, coach of CCNY, was not convinced that the one-hand shot of Hank was the way to play winning basketball. Holman, a hard-bitten character, was a member of the original Celtics.

The next day's *New York Times* gave credit where credit was due—reporting that some of Luisetti's heaves would have looked foolish if attempted by someone else, but with Luisetti shooting, they were accepted by the enchanted crowd. It was not long before nearly every schoolboy in New York was shooting one-handers.

There was no National Basketball Association in those days, for Hank would easily have been offered a fat contract. But his hoop publicity paid off in other ways. Stories in the *Saturday Evening Post* and *Colliers Magazine* helped to make him a national figure.

And perhaps you guessed the next chapter. Hank was in the movies. And believe it or not, he played opposite Betty Grable in her first picture *Campus Confessions*. For his role in that film, Hank received the huge sum of $10,000—only $400 of which was taxable. For that financial gain he was suspended for one year from the Amateur Athletic Union.

Luisetti told a west coast scribe that he began tossing up one-handers like a shot put as a young-ster on the playgrounds because he was so small. "I was too little to get the ball up there any other way—by high school, it was instinctive," he explained.

In 1976 Howie Dallmar, ex-Stanford player and coach, said, "No one I knew, I mean no one, was as far ahead of his contemporaries as Hank was of his.

He was at least twenty years ahead of his time. The guy revolutionized the game."

Following his suspension, Hank played two seasons of AAU ball with the San Francisco Olympic Club and the Phillips 66ers of Oklahoma before joining the Navy. As a member of the St. Mary's College Preflight five, he was at the top of his game, outperforming colleagues such as Jim Pollard, another Stanford product who later became a pro.

He contracted spinal meningitis before shipping out on the Bonhomme Richard in 1944. With the use of sulfur drugs he recovered but was informed his basketball days were over.

If he couldn't play, he could coach and he led the Stewart Chevrolet Company quintet of San Francisco to the Amateur Athletic Union championship in 1951 before retiring. He later turned down a coaching offer from Stanford.

Jerry West, now retired Los Angeles Lakers great, was one of the NBA stars whom Hank enjoyed watching. "I like to think that's the way I'd be if I were back today," he said.

Luisetti, who was also recognized as the first player to dribble and pass behind his back, was inducted into the Bay Area Sports Hall of Fame in March of 1980 along with Joe DiMaggio, Willie

Mays, Bill Russell and Ernie Nevers. DiMaggio and Mays were baseball stars, of course; Russell came out of San Francisco University to make basketball history with the Boston Celtics, and Nevers was an outstanding fullback at Stanford under the late Pop Warner and later starred professionally.

Springfield College coach John Bunn, who tutored Luisetti at Stanford, told Jack Tubert of the *Worcester Telegram* in 1951 that "Hank Luisetti was the greatest player I ever saw—he could have made any team, college or professional, in the United States—even if he never took a shot at the basket."

Bunn recalled Stanford scoring 50, 60, 70 and even 80 points in a game when team totals rarely went over 30 or 40. He also recounted how Hank netted thirteen points in a row to trim CCNY and how a *New York Times* columnist rated Hank "the best basketball player these eyes have ever seen . . . no one could match the 6'3", 185-pounder as a dribbler."

Hank, who always played well against big rival Southern California, rallied his mates from a fifteen-point deficit with eight minutes left, Bunn remembered. "He personally accounted for twenty-four points in those eight minutes—grabbing the ball off either backboard—and passing off for three more field goals . . . We won by three . . . and the crowd mobbed him."

Hank fittingly enough had the pleasure of meeting the man who invented basketball, Dr. James Naismith. The meeting was in 1937, and the rules had been changed to eliminate the center jump after each basket, Luisetti recalled to a San Francisco scribe. It seems Dr. Naismith didn't like the change and was far from impressed with Luisetti's one-handed shot.

Courtesy of Stanford University

So much for change!

Basketball has changed a lot since his day. Luisetti freely admits that the size and mobility of big men is something to behold. In his day a 6'6" player was considered a giant. Now seven-footers are around.

Apparently, competition brought out the best in Hank. As a sophomore against USC he scored eighty-two points in five games, sixty-three in four games as a junior and sixty-nine in four games during his senior year.

Unfortunately, Luisetti's Stanford clubs never had a chance to play for the national crown. The NCAA Championship Tournament first began in 1939, the year after Hank graduated.

For the record, in the fifty-point game against Duquesne in Cleveland, Luisetti benched himself with five minutes left when he realized his teammates were concentrating on feeding him instead of trying to score themselves.

When the Associated Press conducted a poll on the game's great players of the first half of the twentieth century, Hank Luisetti came in second to George Mikan, even though most of the writers and coaches who voted had never seen Luisetti play.

A bronze statue of Luisetti stands outside Mapel Pavilion, home of the Stanford basketball team. Luisetti, who is in his late eighties, is the greatest living athletic immortal of the 1930s. He lives in Foster City, only a few miles up the road from Stanford's Palo Alto campus.

These days, Luisetti never attends a game. "I had a heart bypass about ten years ago," he said. "I watch games only on television now. I prefer that because the excitement of the crowd is too much for me."

Photo by Ray Martin

Dick Vitale serves as college basketball game and studio analyst for ESPN. Considered to be college basketball's top analyst, he joined ESPN during the 1979-80 season—just after the network was launched in September 1979—following a successful college and pro basketball coaching career.

After coaching at the high school level for East Rutherford (New Jersey) High School from 1964 to 1970, Vitale joined Rutgers University for two years as an assistant coach. He then went on to coach at the University of Detroit from 1973 to 1977, compiling a winning percentage of .722. In April 1977, Vitale was named athletic director at Detroit, and later that year was named the United Fund's Detroit

Man of the Year. Vitale became head coach of the NBA's Detroit Pistons in May 1978, serving one-plus seasons before joining ESPN.

In addition to his college basketball analyst duties for ESPN and ESPN Radio, Vitale also provides commentary on a variety of topics in his "Dick Vitale's Fast Break" segment, which airs on Wednesday evenings during the college basketball season on Sports Center. He has been a college basketball analyst for ABC Sports since 1988 and has covered the NBA Finals and the 1992 Summer Olympics for ABC Radio. In October 1995, he began providing a weekly column for ESPNET Sports Zone on the Internet as well as engaging in regular chat sessions. Also in 1995, he captured a Cable ACE Award for top analyst.

During the college basketball season, 125 radio stations carry his syndicated "Dick Vitale Talking Roundball" program, and he has been a featured guest on more than 150 radio talk shows. In addition, he is a columnist for *Basketball Times* and *Eastern Basketball*, and serves as assistant publisher of *Dick Vitale's College Basketball Magazine*, a college basketball preseason annual. He has also served as a guest columnist for *USA Today* since 1991.

Basketball Times named Vitale one of the Five Most Influential Personalities of 1983. He was voted Sports Personality of the Year by the American Sportswriters Association in 1989, and in 1991 by the NIT Metropolitan Media. In 1995, he was honored by Magic Johnson's Roundball Classic for his outstanding contribution to youth. He also received the Phil Rizzuto "Scooter Award," which honors the most caring broadcaster in the New York City metropolitan area, and the Black Coaches Association Honor Award for dedication to youth.

In addition, he's been selected for six halls of fame: the National Italian American Sports Hall of Fame, the Elmwood Park (New Jersey) Hall of Fame (his hometown), the Sarasota Boys and Girls Club Hall of Fame (inducted in the inaugural class of

2001), the University of Detroit Hall of Fame, the Florida Sports Hall of Fame in 1996 (he's a resident of the state), and the East Rutherford (New Jersey) Hall of Fame in 1985.

Born on June 9, 1939, in East Rutherford, New Jersey, Vitale graduated from Seton Hall with a Bachelor of Science degree in business administration. He also earned a master's degree in education from William Paterson College. He and his wife Lorraine have two daughters, Terri and Sherri, who both attended Notre Dame on tennis scholarships, and who both graduated with MBAs.

The Vitale's proud involvement with Notre Dame includes the endowment of the Dick Vitale Family Scholarship, presented annually to an Irish undergraduate who participates in Notre Dame sports or activities and does not receive financial aid. Recipients have included the school's Leprechaun mascot, cheerleaders and band members.

Vitale is also quite a philanthropist. For many years he has awarded annual scholarships to the Boys and Girls Club of Sarasota, Florida. His involvement with the organization was highlighted in April 1999 with the "Dick Vitale Sports Night," a sports memorabilia charity auction which raised thousands of dollars. In recognition of Vitale's support for the Boys and Girls Club, the club named a new building The Dick Vitale Physical Education and Health Training Center.

"I'm living the American Dream," Vitale says. "I learned from my mom and dad, who didn't have formal educations, but had doctorates of love. They told me that if you gave 110 percent all the time, a lot of beautiful things will happen. I may not always be right, but no one can ever accuse me of not having a genuine love and passion for whatever I do."

Carnesecca

ou Carnesecca wasn't much of a basketball player growing up in his native New York—baseball was his game. In fact, the highlight of Lou's college basketball career was playing in three games on the 1946-47 St. John's University jayvee basketball team.

Lou Carnesecca was born January 5, 1925, on the Italian East Side of Manhattan. Lou's dad, like most Italian fathers of the 1930s and 1940s, wanted Lou to learn to play the accordion so he could entertain guests who came for a visit, but Lou had other ideas, so instead he learned to play the clarinet. And instead of going to college to become a doctor as his father had hoped, he became one of the all-time great college basketball coaches.

One night, while speaking at the Sons of Italy Scholar-Athlete banquet in Worcester, Massachusetts, Lou spoke of his days in East Manhattan and what happened one night when he and his mother left a movie theater. "My mother and I had just left the theater and we heard gun shots. She tossed me on the floor of the car while the shooting continued. When the shooting stopped, we drove home."

Carnesecca, who liked to call himself the "Italian Leprechaun," spent a half year at Fordham University where he was enrolled in pre-med before entering St. John's University where he played second base on the baseball team. The coach of both the basketball and baseball teams was the legendary Frank McGuire who had a nickname for Carnesecca, Louie the Lunch, because he enjoyed eating salami sandwiches during games.

Carnesecca's heart, though, was not in baseball but in basketball. During basketball season Lou would attend practice and follow McGuire around asking questions. McGuire decided to hand Lou a whistle and allow him to referee games. McGuire figured that anyone who loved basketball and showed the interest that Carnesecca did would someday become a good coach.

After his 1950 graduation, Lou's first coaching job was at St. Ann's Academy in New York City. He led the school to three national Catholic high school championships in seven seasons. In 1957, St. John's coach Joe Lapchick hired Lou as an assistant. Lou took over as head coach of the Redmen in 1967.

For more than two decades, Lou patrolled basketball sidelines like few others. His supporters talk about him with great reverence and admiration; he has no detractors.

The animated and highly energetic Carnesecca is a New York legend, leading everyone of his St. John's teams to a postseason appearance: 18 NCAAs and 6 NITs. His 1985 Redmen team advanced to the Final Four and the 1979 and 1991 teams competed in NCAA Regional Finals.

In an illustrious coaching career, Carnesecca became the thirtieth coach in NCAA history to reach the 500 victory mark when St. John's defeated Seton Hall, 81-65 on February 2, 1991.

In 1992, Carnesecca was inducted into the Basketball Hall of Fame. In twenty-four seasons as head coach (1967-70, 1973-1992), he had 18 twenty-win seasons and averaged 22 wins a year. The man who made

Courtesy of St. John's University

Carnesecca on the sidelines.

colored sweaters a wardrobe staple retired with a career record of 526-200.

In 1983 and 1985, the United States Basketball Writers Association and the National Association of Basketball Coaches (NABC) named Carnesecca the National Coach of the Year. He was named Big East Coach of the Year in 1983, 1985, and 1986 and he was voted Kodak NIT Man of the Year in 1985. He was also a five-time Metropolitan Coach of the Year.

From 1970 to 1973, Carnesecca coached the New Jersey Nets of the ABA, taking the Nets to the 1972 finals.

Lou retired from coaching following the 1991-1992 season and has remained active at the university. Currently, he is vice president of community

Carnesecca

affairs, assisting the university president. Lou is a member of the New York City Sports Hall of Fame. He was inducted into the National Italian American Sports Hall of Fame in 1996.

Rubini

When Cesare Rubini was elected to the Basketball Hall of Fame, bold headlines of his achievement blazed across newspapers in his native Italy. For the native son who had given five decades of his life to the establishment, structure, refinement, and advancement of Italian basketball, it was a huge announcement. The man who put Italian basketball on the international map was finally being recognized.

Simply stated, Cesare Rubini has been synonymous with Italian basketball. As a player and a coach from 1941 to 1978, he methodically built the Simmenthal Club of Milan and Italian basketball from scratch and tirelessly made Italian basketball an international contender. During his tenure, Rubini won fifteen Italian Basketball Championships, five as a player (1950–55) and ten as a coach. In thirty-one years as head coach of the Simmenthal Club, Rubini compiled an incredible 322-28 record. A graduate of the University of Trieste, Rubini has been a member of FIBS's Central Board since 1984, and has served as president of the World Association of Basketball Coaches since 1979. As a member of the Italian Olympic Water Polo team, Rubini won a Gold Medal at the 1948 Olympics and a Bronze Medal at the 1952 Games.

AUTO RACING

I n 1925, Peter DePaolo became the first man to exceed 100 mph at the Indianapolis 500. Ralph DePalma, who came to the United States from Italy in 1897, earned universal recognition as one of the all-time great drivers in American automobile racing. He gained even greater honors in the nation's early road races and enjoyed almost equal success on the dirt and road tracks, as well as on the sand at Daytona Beach.

Mario Andretti, in twenty-eight years of racing, won races in just about anything that can be driven.

Andretti remembers with special delight teaming up with fellow Italian-American Andy Granatelli to win the Indy 500 in 1964.

DePalma, DePaolo, Andretti, and Granatelli are all National Italian American Sports Hall of Fame enshrinees.

D onald Davidson of the Indianapolis Speed Way said, "I'm not normally one for rating drivers, but I would say that for the period up to about the mid-1920s in this country, DePalma stood out above all of the others. At Indianapolis alone, his record of 612 laps led (between 1911 and 1921) looked as if it was going to last forever and remained unbroken for sixty-six years until it was finally surpassed in 1987 by Al Unser."

Ralph DePalma was so great that his brother John—there were also Frank and Tony—who apparently had very little racing talent, enjoyed a long career as a driver largely because of the relationship. Ralph DePalma was so great that in a 25-year career he won an estimated 2,000 races, including the

Vanderbilt Cup, the Savannah Grand Prize, the Elgin Trophy, and the Indianapolis 500. He won races on dirt tracks, board tracks, speedways, and road courses in many different cars.

The greatness of the man was exemplified by his most famous loss and by his most serious accident. The drama of DePalma and riding mechanic Rupert Jeffkins pushing the famed "Grey Ghost" Mercedes toward the finish (and disqualification) in the 1912 Indianapolis 500 as Joe Dawson whizzed by toward victory in his blue National probably did more to establish the 500 as a premier race than if Ralph had won.

Part of his greatness was his sense of sportsmanship. After the 1913 Indy, when DePalma was sidelined by mechanical ills after thirteen laps in his Mercer, a *Motor Age* correspondent quoted him as saying (before it became a cliche), "It's the luck of the game."

To condense the correspondent's report: "On the glorious afternoon of August 31, 1912, when Ralph DePalma won the Elgin National Trophy—in a car over which he had but partial control—the clutch plate of the Grey Ghost was cracked—E.C. Patterson, entrant of the Mercedes-Knight said, 'DePalma is a popular winner because he is a good loser.' No doubt Patterson is thinking of last Memorial Day. No doubt he sees . . . DePalma pushing his disabled car, a vanquished challenger in a race conceded to him without question ten miles from the finish . . . with face dripping perspiration, DePalma rolls his car over the wire, raises his handsome head and smiles at the cheering throng. DePalma is a man. He does not cry or curse his luck when beaten. DePalma is a sportsman. He is the first to grab the hand of Dawson."

There was an even more compelling example of this sense of fair play—Ralph's most serious accident, which came near Milwaukee in the 1912 Grand Prize road race. He had won the Vanderbilt Cup over the same course a few days before. Attempting to overtake Caleb Bragg, DePalma crashed on the last lap. As he was being carted out to

DePalma

the ambulance bleeding profusely and injured internally, DePalma told reporters, "Boys, don't forget that Caleb Bragg wasn't to blame. He gave me all the road." That and other incidents placed DePalma among the most popular drivers ever. No matter how much they tried to best him, foes honored him as a sportsman. DePalma competed in ten Indy 500s, the last in 1925. He had strong feelings about the posture of a racing hero, saying he owed the crowd the best race he could give. In addition, he was punctilious about honoring appearances, and his entire racing operation was impeccable, serving as the model for others in those rough and ready days.

All of this didn't mean that DePalma wasn't a fearsome competitor. Born in 1883 in Italy and an 1893 arrival in the United States, he was recognized as dirt track king from 1908 through 1911, was the national champion in 1912 and 1914, and the Canadian champion in 1929 after he had forsaken places like Indianapolis for his first love, the dirt ovals. As late as 1936 he was still setting records in stock cars.

With a career like that, it would be presumptuous to pick out one race and call it Ralph's greatest. Ralph saved everyone the trouble. His greatest race, he said, was beating Barney Oldfield in the February 27, 1914, Vanderbilt Cup over the roads of Santa Monica. The Oldfield-DePalma rivalry was one of the greatest in sports history—and one of the most lucrative. Ralph did not let personal feelings stand in the way of an intermittent series of match races that earned large amounts of money for all concerned. Yet the circumstances leading up to the 1914 Vanderbilt Cup would have made perfect strangers the bitterest of rivals.

Early in 1913 DePalma had accepted captaincy of the Mercer factory team, supervising development and construction of three 450-cubic-inch racers. As in most cases, the first year turned out to be a year of correcting weaknesses, a year of hard work and much disappointment. With a relief drive from

DePalma, one Mercer finished second at Indy, but it was a smaller 300-cubic-inch car. All the 450 cars broke down, as they did at Elgin and every stop except Brighton Beach, New York, where DePalma won a 100-mile race. Testing early in 1914, however, showed the 450s finally were ready—one ran 117 miles per hour on a straight. But with about thirty days left before the Vanderbilt Cup, Mercer executives signed Oldfield on as a driver without even telling their team captain, DePalma. It meant that Spence Wishart or Eddie Pullen, who had worked to perfect the car with him, would be without a ride. It also meant that being Mercer captain meant nothing. The fact that Barney had wangled a princely deal rankled no end. Ralph resigned, swearing vengeance. A Los Angeles paper quoted him as saying, "I would rather beat Oldfield than eat five plates of spaghetti in a row." (In later life he did not remember the quote, noting he always preferred linguini to spaghetti.)

Unable to gain a ride on another factory team on such short notice, DePalma prevailed upon his old friend and sponsor, New Jersey lamp manufacturer E.J. Schroeder, to take the old Grey Ghost out of retirement. More than willing, Schroeder financed complete overhaul and shipment to California. DePalma and the car arrived five days after practice had begun and, on his very first outing, burned a bearing. No suitable bearing metal could be found, and if it had not rained three days in a row, postponing the race, DePalma would have been through then and there. He appeared for practice on February 23 and again burned out a bearing. Oldfield said Ralph would never be near enough even to see him. DePalma was desperate, but, as if by a deus ex machina, a gentleman named Kelly appeared and said he would pay Ralph $200 if the Grey Ghost burned a single bearing made out of his "Kelly's metal." Ralph ordered a full set and finally turned in a qualifying lap forty seconds slower than Barney and his former teammates. He knew he could not compete with

DePalma

Oldfield on sheer speed, so he had to win with strategy, using his knowledge of Oldfield to think of a way to capitalize on the weaknesses of car and driver.

Approximately 125,000 people waited, watched and cheered as the cars started single file a few seconds apart on the approximately eight-mile laps. Wishart, in the Mercer, led the first lap, with teammates Pullen and Oldfield third and fourth respectively; DePalma was well back. On the second lap Pullen led, Wishart was in the pits, finished, and Oldfield was third. DePalma was still well back. On the third go around, Pullen was preparing to lap cars, and Oldfield stayed in third behind Stutz's Gil Anderson; DePalma was not a factor. The field began to string out as the laps piled up but on the seventh, Oldfield gave the "coming in" signal. In the pits, Oldfield was the victim of organized confusion; one pit hand even handed him a fresh cigar when all he wanted was a spare wheel lashed to the car. He dropped to fourth, but regained third two laps later with ease. Meanwhile, attrition had put DePalma in the top five.

On the thirteenth lap Pullen, well out in front, crashed against a stand. Eddie had the race easily won had he eased the pressure on the accelerator pedal, but he could not or would not and he was out now, leaving Oldfield alone for the Mercers. And Barney had to pit again for tires and oil. Anderson was leading, but while Oldfield was pitted, the Grey Ghost passed him for second, DePalma as relaxed as if he were on a pleasure jaunt. On the eighteenth lap Anderson was sidelined by a frozen propeller shaft, and now the battle was joined. Barney had roared back into the fray in fifth place; he gained two places in three laps and, with only eight of fifteen starters left after the Stutz departed, had only DePalma ahead of him. With a much faster car, he came closer and closer. On the back stretch of the twenty-fifth lap he finally passed the Grey Ghost, leading with ten laps to go. But suddenly he could not pull away, DePalma slipstreaming him lap

after lap on the straights, leading Barney slightly on the turns because he took the inside line. Ralph still had not made a pit stop.

DePalma knew he did not have the speed to overtake Oldfield. He could see, however, that Barney's wild driving style had worn rubber like a grinding machine off the left front tire. Would Barney risk a pit stop with only fifty miles to go? It was unlikely; the daredevil knew he had the faster car and the tire just might last. Suddenly, as he led slightly coming off the turn into the main straight—when Oldfield could not help but see—Ralph slowed appreciably, signaling he was going to pit for oil. Oldfield roared ahead at top speed, soon losing sight of the Grey Ghost. Playing it safe, Barney pitted next time around for new rubber, confident he had won. But as he sat there in the pits, there went the Grey Ghost racing past into the lead. DePalma never had stopped, and despite a desperate attempt to catch up, Oldfield could not close the gap.

DePalma's average was a record 75.5 miles per hour, but the most amazing thing about his feat was how closely he had figured the winning pace and the pace needed to force Barney to tire-grinding bursts of speed. Ralph's fastest lap was 6:20.2, while Barney got down to 6:10.8, but DePalma's superb sense of pace

kept him within a second of that 6:20 all thirty-five laps. Ralph took the Elgin laurels away from Mercer in 1914, too, and then won Indy in the Grey Ghost. Ironically, Stutz hired Oldfield away from Mercer before the 1914 Indy race.

In later years DePalma acted as honorary referee for the 500, the final time in 1954. He died two years later.

If it had at least one wheel and any kind of steering mechanism, Mario Andretti, the pride of Nazareth, Pennsylvania, would drive it—and win. In his years of racing, the short, powerful dynamo won about any kind of auto race that had a payoff—from midgets and cart racing to hot rods and stock, sports cars and Indy, and he was given a kiss, drank milk, popped champagne and hugged just about every buxom race queen from here to Ballyhack.

He has an Italian grin that opens his face every time something tickles his fancy, but, as a racer, that visage could have the storms of the Italian Alps breaking thunderclaps when he was crossed, passed or beaten. He was a professional in all ways: he drove

Andretti

forcefully but with craftiness; he could drive a race car to the highest degree of superb performance, and he was the "man to beat" anywhere in any race because of who he was and not necessarily the car he drove.

During his racing days, he once said, "Any car I set up, I know will perform." There was a hint of cockiness, but it was the truth. Having won the Indy, Daytona, 12 Hours of Sebring, and the Formula One World Driving Championship, among many others, his boast was not hollow.

Mario raced against Paul Newman and also raced for him. Their paths crossed many times and Newman holds Mario in awe. And Paul has Mario's respect, as well. "Newman knows what's going on, darn right. He handles his cars like a pro and he never bitches when things go wrong. That's class," Andretti once said.

Andretti is not a complainer either, but in the 1981 Indy, Mario went to bed a second-place loser but woke up a protest-winning champion. Bobby Unser had passed eight cars on a caution lap and the next morning was stripped of his crown.

"Don't forget," Andretti said, "he got all the honors, hoopla, ink and fringe benefits of a winner right after the race ended. That's what I remember most about my '69 Indy win. That's the greatest

ending of any race anywhere. When they named me the protest winner, it was as hollow as a log. That's not how I like to win. I should have won it in my car on the track. Unser should have been penalized right when it happened. I'd have had a full lap on him then."

The decision was again reversed on October 17, 1981 in favor of Unser by an arbitration committee.

During his career, Mario's mother, Rina, always said, "I want him to quit." His dad, Gigi, was another dynamo and a good role model for Mario. Back in the early days, the family car was a Hudson.

"I was competing in an unsanctioned race on a local street and flipped the Hudson on its back," Mario recalled. "The only trouble was we were supposed to trade it in the next day for a '57 Chevy."

They eventually got the Chevy, but Gigi had to keep his nose to the grindstone at Bethlehem Steel to swing it.

"For years," said Gigi, "there was red paint on that tree he hit. I'd go by and think of Mario and then I would say, 'There is an angel flying over that boy.'"

As a competitor, Mario thrived on attention, and he got a lot of it. When he drove one of Newman's cars, fans would flock to him, drawn by the Newman-Andretti connection. When fans would question him about championship races, the gregarious Mario would tell them, "The biggest thing I've done is that world championship in Formula One. I won the Formula crown six times in six countries. That's more than just one race. I'm not demeaning Indy or Daytona or Riverside or Dallas or Watkins Glen. It's just that the whole series is against the top drivers in the world, and that's something really to be proud of." In 1978, Andretti had the distinction of being the second American driver to win the Formula One World Driving Championship. Phil Hill was the first American to do so in 1961.

On character building: "Top competition just has to build character. You dial in your car as perfectly as you can, the mechanics set it up as perfectly as they can and you race as perfectly as you can, and a tire blows, a nut falls off a wheel and the damn thing comes flying over your head, a block cracks or a line spews gas or oil when it gets dislodged, punctured or too hot. Your world collapses and you'd like to kill someone. It takes character not to."

Andretti was born in Trieste, Italy. Both he and his twin brother Aldo studied automobile mechanics, frequented racing-car garages, and participated in a race-driving training program in Italy before his family moved to America when he was fifteen years old.

On his arrival, he spoke no English, and he had trouble trying to compete in school. He took a job at a filling station after school, where he picked up the language by talking with customers.

At the station, a mecca for all sorts of automobiles, Mario fell in love with foreign cars, which he had raced in Italy. He worked on them and memorized every facet of their construction.

His family came to the United States in 1955. By 1958, the brothers were racing stock cars.

Mario Andretti

Aldo was severely injured in an accident and gave up racing after 1959. In the early 1960s, Mario drove sprint and midget cars in races, and in 1964 (the year he became a United States citizen) he began racing in the championship division of the United States Automobile Club (USAC). He won USAC championships in 1965, 1966, and 1969. He also won the Daytona Beach 500-mile stock-car race in 1967 and the sports-car Grand Prix of Endurance race at Sebring, Florida in 1967 and 1970. He had a feel for whatever he drove and would become one with the machine. He was not the most popular driver among drivers, but he was the most respected driver all over the world.

Andretti once summed up his career this way: "I've won races on 127 different kinds of tracks, and I

Andretti

don't think there's anyone who can match me. And that includes going both ways, starting right and starting left. I've seen the engines go from the front to the back, I won in stock cars in NASCAR, Indy-type in the big U.S. circuit, formula cars all over the world, sports cars on every kind of track. I lived for racing and being able to drive. I have my life at home in Nazareth with my family and all my friends back there. Man, when you love what you're doing, you don't need hobbies."

A.J. Foyt, the irascible old coot who caused more waves than the moon, was once asked if Andretti was free of commitments to sponsors would Foyt like to add him to his stable of drivers.

"I've said it before," Foyt bellowed, "and I'll say it again. If I had to pick another guy to drive for me, it would be the Wop." Then he added, "But who'd be damn fool enough to let him get free?"

If anyone thought they owned Mario, they had another thought coming. As an active driver, he said, "I know what team racing is, but I'm fiercely independent. I don't want anyone doing my job. I am comfortable when I do it myself. I feel confident if I've personally checked everything on the car. I feel I contribute 110 percent to myself. This means success in most cases—winning."

Andretti always wanted to win, always wanted to be respected for his skill of driving and always wanted to be successful in life. He accomplished all three goals with plenty of room to spare.

But there is one major feeling he gets when all the above are considered, especially as it refers to his racing ability.

In cities all over the world, Mario can walk the street, enter a restaurant or be seen on TV, and he is still readily recognized and respected. In Europe, especially, there is a class to racing champions; they are respected and honored, sort of like yachtsmen on the East Coast.

Maximum speed was the only thing Andretti ever found elusive. He sought it since his youth in Trieste, his days working on the Hudson at the garage, and his years in every racing machine from midgets to monsters. He sped faster than others, won innumerable races, but the maximum speed that can possibly be attained by a racer with the best equipment has never been determined and probably never will be, at least not by Mario Andretti.

He retired from competition in 1994.

GOLF

O n July 15, 1922, at Skokie Country Club, in Glencoe, Illinois, Gene Sarazen (Eugenio Saraceni), age twenty and with virtually no competitive credentials, achieved one of the most sensational victories in golf history by winning the U.S. Open Championship. Fifteen years later, the elegant "squire" of golf would become one of only four men to win all four major championships: Masters, U.S. Open, British Open, and P.G.A Championship.

Sarazen opened the door for other great Italian-American golfers to follow, including: Ken Venturi, Donna Caponi, Doug Ford, Fred Couples, Chris DiMarco, and Mark Calcavecchia.

Courtesy of the Worcester Telegram & Gazette

Sarazen

Gene Sarazen was only 5'4" in a game of 6-footers. Golf was the game which took this former caddy out of the caddy shack and into the club house and made his name honored all over the world.

The son of an Italian immigrant father who picked up the carpentry trade, he was born Gene Saraceni in 1902. "I changed it to McSarazen so I would sound Scottish. I didn't have to keep it very long."

Hit by a siege of pneumonia as a youth of ten, doctors told him he would have to get out doors more, and, if possible, work outside.

"My father wanted me to join him in the carpentry business, but I had no heart for it. The only thing open to me was a golf course and caddying. I used to get 35 or 40 cents per round, but I had a chance to play with borrowed clubs when the course was empty, very early, or after the last golfer finished number 18. Sometimes, I'd start out after they had gone only four or five holes and keep out of sight."

He got his first break when he chose to winter in Florida in 1919. He played golf every day and landed an assistant pro job at the Fort Wayne (Indiana) Country Club. "The members," Sarazen recalled, "chipped in to send me to Inverness (Toledo) for my first Open. I finished thirtieth, but at least I got my feet wet." Early in 1922, he decided to play the winter tour of the PGA and won the Southern Open.

"I picked up a bit of respect after that win. I won a new assignment at Highland Country Club in Pittsburgh as head pro. I was proud of that. Filled with a lot of confidence, I went to Shokie [Illinois] and won my first PGA Open, on my third attempt. I was only twenty years old at the time, but what I remember is that I shot dead on the last hole for a record sixty-eight round and edged out the immortal Bobby Jones for the title."

Sarazen's golf world opened up like a rose in the sunshine. "I beat Walter Hagen for the 1922 PGA title and again in 1923, so I had won three major titles in slightly more than a year. But my world collapsed for about four or five years," he said. "Somehow I lost my swing. I just couldn't get into my groove. Every person who talked with me told me what I was doing wrong, but, frankly, no two said the same thing.

"I became a confident trap player only after I invented the sand-iron. The club . . . was born in a small machine shop in New Port Richey late in 1931. I was trying to make myself a club that would drive the ball *up* as I drove the clubhead *down*. When a pilot wants to take off, he doesn't raise the tail of his plane, he lowers it. Accordingly, I was lowering the tail or sole of my niblick to produce a club whose face would come up from the sand as the sole

Sarazen

made contact with the sand. I experimented with soldering various globs of lead along the sole of my niblick until I arrived at a club that had an exceptionally heavy, abrupt, wide, curving flange. I [hit] thousands of shots each week, making adjustments back in the machine shop, texting the improvements until I had the sand-iron perfected."

Sarazen kept his club under wraps, showing it to nobody. He went over to the British Open. Here's how he recounted it:

"I made sure no one saw the club until after the championship started. On the first five or six holes, I was in a trap two or three times. I whipped out the club and played the ball right out of the trap aiming for the cup.

"The British started saying, 'By Jove, have you seen this weapon Sarazen has?' By that time, it was too late to do anything about the club, they couldn't rule it out, and it hasn't been ruled out since. That was the birth of the sand blaster [wedge] and it has been a boon to players ever since.

"It made golfing easier for the average golfer as well as the pro. A majority of the players never could play that shot too well. Hagen never played a good sand shot and neither did Jones. They both used to chip it out of the sand, thankful to get it out—period."

Sarazen had a reputation for being close with a buck. One time he won a tournament in Agua Caliente and they delivered 10,000 silver dollars to him in a wheel barrow. "One thing is sure," one of them said, "Gene still has those silver dollars." Hagen, who loved the little guy, added, "He still has the wheelbarrow!"

As close as Gene was with the coin of the realm, he had a deep, abiding love for caddies. He never forgot the third-class citizenship status they worked under, even though they were responsible for improving the games of many members by giving advice on distance, club selection, and how to best handle a given situation.

"Practically all the champions were former caddies—myself, Hagen, Francis Ouimet, Chick Evans,

Sarazen

who founded the scholarship program for caddies; Byron Nelson, Sam Snead, Ben Hogan and you can name hundreds more. Too many country clubs offer no facilities for them. Before World War II, there were almost one million youngsters who were carrying or had carried golf bags for a living, for spending money or college tuition. This is why the modern pro making the big money respects the caddy and pays him well for his important services," Gene said. "Club golfers who still don't ride carts should be respectful to their caddies."

A classic swing.

Sarazen

With Sarazen, you have to think of two great shots and a third that no one knows about.

The first might be the final hole of the Skokie PGA Open. As Gene said, "I'll never forget the minute I stood on the 18th green at Skokie, figuring that a four might win. It was a tough four, over 450 yards. I hit a fine drive and planted a long brassie shot just twelve feet from the cup. I almost got a three. I still beat Jones by a stroke. Not really a great shot, but a great hole.

"A great shot came in on my 38-hole battle with Hagen, for the PGA championship. There was the twelfth hole at Pelham, real tough, and I hit it with my drive nine straight times. But that Hagen, was he tough! I was hitting all the par fives in two for my birdies . . . and he was chipping bird on the 38th. My drive crashed into a tree near the out-of-bounds marker and Hagen's brilliant tee shot stopped just off the green, dead on. I had to play a recovery pitch from grass around my knees, but I got it close—stone dead—while Walter missed his. I felt drained when his putt skidded by."

His second real shot was the only shot most people think Sarazen ever hit. That was the double eagle at Augusta. Gene said he felt that people thought he was born on the fifteenth hole at Jones' backyard course.

"Yes, I got a two on the 510-yard fifteenth, but people don't realize that I was three down to Craig Wood. I knew three birdies on the last four were nigh impossible. But I got all three of them on that pair of shots.

"Sinking that spoon shot, 220 yards away, was a million-to-one shot, I admit that, especially since it was in a drizzling rain, too. When the first roar went up from the crowd, I knew my ball was close. But when I heard a silence and then a roar that tripled with hats flying in the air, I figured the miracle had happened. What a shot!"

Then Sarazen added, grinning, "Know what? Among the people on the green who saw the shot was Bobby Jones. I was playing with Hagen, so having both Jones and Hagen see that shot, that topped the whole glorious day for me."

The shot they didn't see? In 1972, thirty-seven years after the Augusta shot, Gene went to Boston to play for the Francis Ouimet caddy fund at the Charles River Country Club. On the par-five seventh hole, he sank his second shot for a double eagle. He used a 3-wood.

"What did you hit at Augusta?" he was asked.

"A 4-wood," Sarazen answered. "Since it's thirty-seven years after, I needed more club," he kidded.

Freddie Corcoran, an early player representative, handled Sarazen, Ted Williams and the like. Always the friendly sort, Corcoran called Sarazen for a golf date down at Marco Island, Gene's Florida hideaway. "Naw, Fred," Gene said, "we'll just have lunch together."

When Corcoran arrived there, actually to celebrate Gene's 70th birthday, he told Sarazen, "Gene, I've got an idea. Let's play. We'll announce that anybody who shoots a seventy on February 27, your birthday, gets a free set of Gene Sarazen clubs!"

"Like hell," Sarazen shouted. He never concealed his admiration for solid Italian and American virtues like thrift. "I suppose you want me to pay for their green fees, too, huh?" he added.

Sarazen never complained about the big money the players are making today. He probably stretched his money a lot farther and acquired more property than the fellows now playing can muster.

"I always wanted to sink my roots somewhere. I love the land. I had a nice Connecticut farm, fruit trees and stone walls, but when I was offered a good profit when I had just started making good money in golf, I sold the place. I felt sick afterward, with no property. I felt I had no rights unless I had property. Well, driving up the Hudson one day, I stopped and bought two farms. I felt good again."

How did he keep things in balance after living in both worlds of sport and income? "Ya' know," Sarazen said, "I saw where a fellow got $1,500 for thirtieth place in a general type tournament the other day. I got $500 for winning my first PGA Open!"

"But I have more than he has or ever will have . . . and he'll never understand why."

Gene Sarazen died on May 13, 1999, at age ninety-seven in Naples, Florida.

Sarazen

Gene Sarazen's Record

MAJOR CHAMPIONSHIP VICTORIES

U.S. Open	1922, 1932
P.G.A. Championship	1922, 1923, 1933
British Open	1932
Masters	1935

OTHER TOURNAMENT VICTORIES

Southern Open	1921
North of England Professional Championship	1922, 1927, 1928, 1939
Metropolitan Open	1925, 1927, 1928. 1939
Long Island Open	1927
Miami Four-ball	1928, 1941
Florida West Coast Open	1930, 1931, 1937
La Gorce Open	1930
Agua Caliente Open	1930
Western Open	1930
New Orleans Open	1932
Massachusetts Open	1935
Australian Open	1936
Chicago Open	1937
Lake Placid Open	1938
PGA Seniors' Championship	1954, 1958

OTHER ACHIEVEMENTS

- Second in 1928 British Open, 1930 P.G.A. Championship, and 1934 and 1940 U.S. Open
- Third in 1927 and 1928 U.S. Opens and 1936 Masters.
- Tied third in 1926 and 1929 U.S. Opens and 1931 and 1933 British Opens.
- In 1922 defeated Walter Hagen, 3 and 2, in 72-hole unofficial "World's Golf Championship" match.
- Member of all five U.S. Ryder Cup teams from 1927 to 1937, winning a then record 8.5 points from a possible 12.
- Honorary member of the Royal and Ancient Golf Club of St. Andrews. Member of the Muirfield Village Golf Club Captain's Club.

Sarazen

Courtesy of the Worcester Telegram & Gazette

Caponi

As a child, Donna Caponi dreamed of making the winning putt on the final hole to capture the U.S. Women's Open, but she never imagined the scenario to win her first-ever LPGA tournament in golf's biggest event.

Facing a four-foot putt on the 72nd hole to win the 1969 U.S. Women's Open, as Caponi lined up the crucial putt, she overheard the legendary Byron Nelson commentating on television say, "Donna Caponi has this putt to win the U.S. Women's Open."

Caponi recalls struggling to breathe and to make matters worse, she couldn't believe Nelson's report. "I've been watching this putt all day and it's almost dead straight. It might move slightly to her right."

"I thought," said Caponi, "how can Byron Nelson see this putt break left to right, it's right to left."

Flustered, she backed off the putt to regain her composure. She had already weathered a fifteen-minute delay after hitting her tee shot on 18 when an electrical storm passed through. Now was the moment for which she had waited a lifetime and she questioned her read. Like a true champion, she decided to trust the line and proceeded to coolly sink the right to left putt. "Thank goodness I went with my own instincts."

At the press conference, she learned that Nelson was right after all. It turns out his monitor was showing a camera angle from the opposite direction!

The victory launched a Hall of Fame career spanning 24 years from 1965 to 1988 during which she collected 24 titles and four major championships. While the first U.S. Women's Open title was sweet, joining Mickey Wright as only the second player to defend the championship successfully was even sweeter. "A lot of people know my first win was the U.S. Open. That was a thrill, but winning the second U.S. Open [was the biggest deal]. I knew a lot more the second time around," said Caponi, who also equaled Wright's record score of 287 that week.

Sixteen years after that first major title, she captured her final one at the 1981 LPGA Championship. Again, it was a storybook ending. Caponi rolled in a 25-footer for birdie on the final hole for a one-stroke victory.

Caponi spent the final seasons of her career trying to win six more times to qualify for the Hall of Fame and the pressure took the fun out of the game. She retired in 1992, figuring she would have to settle for two U.S. Opens and two LPGA Championships as her most prized accomplishments.

"I just said the Hall of Fame is not going to happen," she said.

Caponi's hopes for enshrinement were renewed when the LPGA overhauled its criteria for the Hall

of Fame in 1999. The Veteran's Committee, formed in 1999 as part of the new requirements, nominated Caponi in March 2001. She then received the required seventy-five percent of the vote from Tour members. She is the second woman elected to the World Golf Hall of Fame through the LPGA Veteran's category following Judy Rankin, who was selected in 2000. She was inducted into the LPGA Hall of Fame in 2001.

"It just caps off my career, but more than anything, what makes this so meaningful is that it's the players voting for you—your peers voting for you—and knowing they consider you of a quality for the Hall of Fame," said Caponi.

Once she received word of her election, she held back tears talking about her parents—Harry, who died in 1971 at age forty-nine and Dolly, who died of breast cancer in 1986 at fifty-six.

"I owe everything I am today to my parents," said Caponi, who won the Los Angeles Junior title in 1956. "I owe everything to my dad who spent hours and hours and hours teaching me."

Caponi started playing golf at age six and grew up picking up balls with her sister, Jane, at the driving range where her father was head professional.

She recalled how her father took her to the back end of the driving range and had her practice shaping shots around a large avocado tree.

"I always felt each win was for him because he did make me what I am today."

Caponi

SOFTBALL

Back in 1963, Ralph Raymond was not sure he was interested in coaching women's softball. After all, his schedule was pretty full coaching American Legion baseball, high school football and a couple of Men's Major Fast Pitch softball clubs in his hometown of Worcester, Massachusetts.

Born on April 27, 1924, to Antonio and Lydia Raimondi, Raymond was already somewhat of a legend in the city, having captained his high school baseball, football and basketball teams before passing on a promising professional baseball career to pursue his first love of teaching.

But still, Raymond was open to the possibilities, which led to a meeting with a sponsor of a Women's

Raymond

Courtesy of the Worcester Telegram & Gazette

Ralph Raymond cheers his team.

Raymond

Major club from Cochituate, Massachusetts. "When I left for the meeting I wasn't sure I wanted to do that. But I went down to Cochituate and stayed there four years."

From the start, Raymond demonstrated a propensity for winning the big ones. In 1965, his team, Cochituate Motors, was invited to participate in an annual July softball tournament in Stratford, Connecticut, home of the renowned Raybestos Brakettes. "So we went down and we beat them [the Brakettes]," Raymond said.

The win proved to be an important one for Raymond because it resulted in a phone call the following day from William S. Simpson, Chairman of the Board and President of Raybestos. Simpson popped the question and Raymond was on his way to Stratford as an assistant to manager Vin DeVitt.

Two years later, after DeVitt's retirement, Raymond took over the Brakettes and over the next three decades established them as one of the all-time great and enduring sport dynasties, amassing an incredible seventeen national titles and seven runner-up finishes.

In fact, under Raymond's tutelage, the Brakettes have finished out of the top two at the ASA National Championships only twice.

Raymond's career record of 1,992 wins and only 162 losses with the Brakettes is second to none in history. Even the Gipper couldn't insure enough wins for Knute Rockne (105-12-5) to eclipse the Worcester Wrecking Ball. The winning percentages of immortals like Vince Lombardi and baseball's Joe McCarthy (2,126-1,335) were also-rans against Raymond.

In 1994, Raymond wrote the final chapter on his Brakette saga and turned the page that led him into what was, perhaps, his greatest challenge—he was named as first-ever Olympic softball coach for the USA.

At the time of the appointment, he made a solemn promise. "We're going to carry the torch for all the young ladies out there. For the Joanie Joyces, the Bertha Tickeys, the Barbie Reinaldas, the Kathy Arendsens, and all the others who put in their time, hoping some day they'd be able to play in the Olympics. We're kind of like the torch bearers for the young ladies in the past and future," he said.

And if the players are the torch bearers, Raymond was certainly equipped to light the Olympic cauldron.

Raymond's international record was imposing. As head coach of the USA Softball Women's National Team, he has produced five gold medals in ISF World Championship play, including three consecutive (1986, 1990, 1994) for a combined record of 72-1.

He has also produced thirteen other gold medals representing the USA in competitions including the

Pan American Games (1967, 1979, 1995, 1999); World Games (1981, 1985); Intercontinental Cup (1985, 1993); World Cup (1986); Challenger Cup (1992); South Pacific Classic (1994); Superball Classic (1995); and Canada Cup (1999).

In U.S. Olympic Festival competition, he coached the Brakettes to gold medals in 1979, 1986, 1989, 1990 and 1991.

Raymond has managed to associate himself with extraordinary talent. The USA Softball Women's National Team has been so dominating in recent years that it has won every competition in which it has played. Since 1986 they are 110-1 in international play.

For Raymond, being named softball's first Olympic coach was a pinnacle point in his career. But, for him, winning the gold medal meant reaching the top of that mountain.

Raymond's climb was fruitful, as the USA won the gold in 1996 and 2000.

In 2002, Raymond accepted a position as a special consultant to the United States Women's National Team Program.

"I feel like this position will allow me the flexibility to spend more time with my family while still contributing to the USA softball program," he said.

Mary Lou Retton moved into the lime-light at a very young age. In the 1984 Olympic Games in Los Angeles, at the age of sixteen, Mary Lou won five Olympic medals. One of those medals was a gold for the All-Around in which she scored perfect "10"s in the floor exercise and vault. This made her the first American woman ever to win a gold medal in gymnastics. She also won silver medals for Team and Vault, and bronze medals for Uneven Bars and Floor Exercise. Her five medals were the most won by any athlete at the 1984 Olympics. To this day she remains the only American ever to win the Olympic All-Around title.

Mary Lou was born in the small coal-mining town of Fairmont, West Virginia on January 24,

Retton

1968. Her talent at gymnastics was obvious from an early age.

Moving to Houston, Texas, Mary Lou was coached by the renowned Bela Karolyi.

As the 1984 Olympics approached, Mary Lou pushed herself to the limit. And just six weeks before the games were to begin, she broke cartilage in her knee. Surgery was needed, and the doctors told Mary Lou that she would not be able to compete—they were wrong, of course.

With fierce determination, Mary Lou completed three months worth of rehabilitation in only three weeks. Her determination and hard work paid off. She became the best known American gymnast in history.

Other victories include being the only woman to win three American Cups (1983, 1984, 1985); the only American to win Japan's prestigious Chunichi Cup (1983); two U.S. Gymnastic Federation American Classics (1983, 1984); and the All-Around title at both the 1984 National Championships and Olympic Trials. Mary Lou retired from competitive gymnastics in 1986.

Today, she continues to touch the lives of millions. She is in great demand as a motivational speaker and corporate spokesperson and also travels the world as a "Fitness Ambassador" promoting the benefits of proper nutrition and regular exercise. Mary Lou serves as national chairperson and sits on the Board of Governors of the Children's Miracle Network. She was a commentator for NBC at the 1988 Olympic Games and wrote a daily column for *USA Today* at the 1992 and 1996 Olympics. At the 1996 Olympics in Atlanta, Mary Lou also served as an on-air reporter for Gannett Broadcasting's NBC affiliates—the largest NBC affiliate group in the United States. In addition, she co-hosted the weekly television series "Road to Olympic Gold."

Mary Lou has also added acting credits to her career. She appeared in the motion pictures *Scrooge* and *Naked Gun 33⅓*. She has made appearances on numerous television shows including "Guiding

Retton

Light," "Knots Landing" and "Dream On," and guest starred in one of the highest rated episodes of the series "Baywatch."

Many awards and honors have been bestowed on Mary Lou including 1984 *Sports Illustrated* Sportswoman of the Year; 1984 Associated Press amateur Athlete of the Year; the first gymnast and youngest inducted into the USOC Olympic Hall of Fame; the first woman to appear on the Wheaties box; and one of America's Top Ten "Most Admired" public figures.

In 1994 the U.S. Olympic Committee established the annual Mary Lou Retton Award for athletic excellence. In 1995, First Lady Hillary Rodham Clinton presented Mary Lou with the Flo Hyman Award in recognition for her spirit, dignity and commitment to excellence. Mary Lou was selected as a member of the official White House delegation representing the President at both the 1992 and 1998 Olympic Games.

She was elected to the National Italian American Sports Hall of Fame in 1992.

Mary Lou and her husband, former University of Texas quarterback Shannon Kelley, live in Houston with their two children.

Courtesy of Manhattan College

L indy Remigino, the cinderella winner of the 100-meter dash in the 1952 Olympic Games at Helsinki, Finland was well named. His immigrant Italian parents named him for Charles Lindbergh, who became an international hero after becoming the first transatlantic aviator to fly solo from New York to Paris.

In that era, many affectionately referred to Lindbergh as "Lucky Lindy." Lindy Remigino was a surprise winner of the century in Finland as he leaned across the tape to nose out Herb McKenley, the University of Illinois ace who was representing Jamaica. Both were timed in 10.4 seconds and the ever-modest Remigino walked over to congratulate Herb who he thought had won in a real photo finish.

Remigino

The camera, however, revealed that the Manhattan College junior from Hartford, Connecticut, had captured the gold medal. Lindy was a stunned but delighted victor after the press had mobbed him.

The Official Olympic Souvenir Program of the 1984 games at Los Angeles gives Lindy's version of that memorable day in Helsinki:

A 32 year-old wound to the ego can still fester, especially if it scars the memory of an Olympic triumph. Lindy Remigino, now a successful high school track coach in Hartford, Connecticut, wants it known that his victory in the 100-meter sprint in the Helsinki Games in 1952 was no fluke and he was no "Cinderella Kid," as the newspapers called him. "It bothers me because it sounds like I came out of the woodwork," he said. Here's the way Lindy remembers it:

"Jim Golliday was our best American hope for a gold, but he got hurt. Andy Stanfield passed up the 100 for the 200; Barney Ewell and Mel Patton had retired; and Art Bragg broke down in a semifinal heat.

"I'm no dummy. I saw all this happening and I was gaining confidence. Herb McKenley from Jamaica and Emmanuel McDonald Bailey from Britain were the favorites, but I didn't feel like an underdog. In the first trial heat Remigino wins easily. In the second trial heat, it was the same thing. [McKenley nosed out Remigino in a semifinal heat.]

"Then I'm in the finals and I'm out in front at 80 meters and I want to win so much that I do something that is strate-

Remigino

gically bad—I start leaning to the damn tape. I gave it the Madison Square Garden lean like I'd done in all those 60-yard dashes at the Garden and this shortened my stride. I hear McKenley coming up—chuka-chuka-chuk—and I felt the tape, but he went by me and I thought he had won and I go over to congratulate him. Then the names go up on the board and boom—it's Remigino USA—first. And then I'm on the victory stand. Here I am the skinny, little guy from the Bronx with meatball eyes, and they give me a gold medal.

"They called me the Cinderella Kid, and it stuck. But—and this is important—I ran against those guys in Europe after the Games and I beat them. I won everything.

"You know, I saw McKenley in Montreal in 1976 and we joked about it; we said we'd meet on the track at noon and have it out, once and for all. But I didn't show up and I found later that he didn't show up either."

To prove his point, Lindy along with other USA stars, competed in several major competitions en route home. He won the 100 and 220-yard events in the British World Games in 1952 and 1954. He took the 100 in the 1952 and 1954 Scottish Games, captured the 100-meter special sprint in 1952 in Amsterdam and equaled the world record of 10.2 in winning the Oslo, Norway 100-meter special sprint.

Not to be overlooked. Lindy was a member of the United States 100x4 relay team which took the gold medal at Helsinki.

Remigino

Courtesy of Manhattan College

At the Knights of Columbus meet in 1952 (left to right): John O'Connell, Joe Schatzel, an unidentified runner from Morgan State University, and Lindy Remigino.

He warmed up for the Olympics the previous winter by taking the sixty-yard dash in both the famed Millrose Games at Madison Square Garden and the New York Knights of Columbus Games.

Lindy, who ran on many of the late George Eastmen's outstanding relay teams at Manhattan, was admitted to the Manhattan Hall of Fame in 1979. The citation reads in part: "High on Mount Olympus stands modest, loyal Lindy Remigino, the 'World's Fastest Human;' Manhattan's first and only champion of the Gold in the international track games at Helsinki, Finland, July, of 1952."

Remigino

Courtesy of Manhattan College

Manhattan's famous sprint relay team of 1951 and 1952 after winning the 440 and 880 titles at the Penn Relays (left to right): Joe Schatzel, John O'Connell, Lindy Remigino, and Bob Carty.

Remigino

In the West Coast trials Lindy was shooting for berths in both the 100 and 200 meters. He fought an uphill fight to make the team in 100, but literally cooked his chances for the 200 by exposing himself too long in the California sun. As fate would have it, he was considered a stronger runner in the 200. Lindy qualified for the Olympic trials with a fifth place finish in the NCAA 100. And only ten weeks before Helsinki he considered quitting track after a disappointing loss at West Point.

Upon returning to Hartford later where

he received a hero's welcome, Lindy inaugurated a series of summer track meets under the auspices of the Parks Department—a contribution to track which has assisted many a hopeful. It was a community gesture typical of a modest man who had scaled the heights of stardom.

Remigino

Courtesy of the Worcestser Telegram and Gazette

Arcaro

The heart. How does one account for the fact that an organ the size of a fist, weighing a half to three quarters of a pound, does enough power work each day to lift the body a mile straight up?

Certainly George Edward Arcaro, born February 19, 1916 in Cincinnati, Ohio had a special heart, for he displayed the fortitude and skills at 114 pounds to boot home 4,779 winning twelve-hundred pound running machines in a thirty-year professional career.

Imagine surviving thirty years in a field in which you know each race may be your last, because the risk of being thrown or trampled by another horse is so great. A horse breaking a leg is like losing the front wheel of a motorcycle at forty miles per hour. Each year two hundred and fifty riders suffer serious injuries. By 1982, nearly fifty paraplegic riders, including Secretariat's former rider, Ron Turcotte, were receiving disability payments from the Jockey's Guild. In the past two decades more than twenty riders have been killed in racing accidents. Incidentally, none other than Eddie Arcaro served as president of the Jockey Guild from 1949 to 1961. It was in that capacity that Arcaro, when confronted with the case of an indigent rider with family problems, quickly commanded the Guild treasurer to "reach in the drawer and give him five big ones [$5,000]." He knew that it could have been him just as easily.

Said Arcaro, "There were plenty of times when I was afraid. Every day something would come up that would give me a scare. But I figured that when I signed my name to be a jockey that death might be a part of it. Every jockey should know that or get out. Jockeys know what hard competition is, and in racing, if you want to make it real big you can't be afraid of dying! That day I fell from Black Hills didn't bother me. You couldn't have put a gun into my back then and made me stop riding. I didn't think the injury was that serious." The fall from Black Hills took place in the Belmont Stakes on June 13, 1959, and was serious enough to cause Arcaro's father to suffer a heart attack right in the stands.

Eddie Arcaro was serious about his riding. His competitive fires carried him to the top of his profession. Baron Fred d'Osten, an internationally known racing authority, was once quoted as saying, "Since 1920, I have seen all the top jockeys ride in countries throughout the world; men such as Steve Donoghue, Sir Gordon Richards, Charley Eliot, Earl Sande, Roger Poincelet, Rae Johnstone and many others. Arcaro is far superior to any of them."

As an athlete Arcaro ranks with Dempsey, Ruth, Jones, Tilden and Marciano. As a jockey, no one can be considered close to him and although purses have increased and will continue to increase, no rider will ever unseat him as the top stakes jockey of all time. His record of 4,779 winners has been passed, as has

his money-earning record of $30,039,543. But the record of 549 stakes won may stand forever. Arcaro also won an astounding total of 17 Triple Crown races.

Sometimes Eddie's competitiveness got him in trouble, as his frequent suspensions will attest. He started as a stable boy at thirteen. He was soon exercising race horses and rode in his first race on May 18, 1931, at the old Bainbridge Park near Cleveland. Arcaro rode his first winner at Agua Caliente on January 14, 1932, one month shy of his sixteenth birthday. Alvin Booker gave Eddie a leg up on Eagle Bird, saying, "This is it. Get home first the best way you know how." Eagle Bird flew home with young Arcaro bouncing up and down on him and grinning from ear to ear.

In the spring of 1933 he went to Chicago and soon acquired a reputation as an "infant terrible." He was brought up to believe the Leo Durocher quote that "nice guys finish last." Nothing was barred: straight-arming another jockey, grabbing an opponent's saddle cloth, or locking legs with the jockey alongside to throw him off balance. Before the days of the Patrol cameras, these tactics were common, for if you could be intimidated you would be sent quickly packing for home. So Arcaro had to learn early on to give no quarter. Over the years he mellowed, but he never lost his competitive drive and was often suspended for rough riding.

One famous instant occurred when Eddie was suspended in September 1942 for the rest of that year and for most of 1943. In Eddie's own words, "I tried to put a Cuban jockey named Vincent Nordase over the rails at the old Aqueduct. He cut me off at the gate on a horse called Occupation. I saw red and shot out after him and Breezing Home, and every time I went to knock him over the fence his horse kept stumbling and I couldn't get to him. When the race was over, the stewards called me up and old man Woodward said, 'Son, what were you trying to do out there?' I said, 'I was trying to kill that Cuban so and so.' I got suspended for a year, and every month I'd have to go before the stewards and plead my case to try to get back riding. But for some reason or another they had a record device in the stewards' room that day, and old man Woodward would turn it on and I'd hear myself saying again that 'I was trying to kill that Cuban so and so.' and I didn't have a chance of getting back. Old Mrs. Payne Whitney, she was the one that saved me. She let me go to Aiken for Greentree and paid me $1,000 a month to work her horses. Every few weeks she'd send me a check for $500 so I'd have some money to spend. Young Carolyn was just about to be born, and Ruth and I didn't have much money. She wrote a letter to Mr. Woodward and I still have it. It said, 'Dear Bill, I know you try to do the best for everyone, but the one thing I want to see before I die is to see Eddie ride again.' And he let me, and it changed my whole life. It made me obey the rules, and it made me realize what being nice to people means."

Amidst injury, Arcaro spent the next six years charting his course as a top jockey.

In 1938, Arcaro won his first Kentucky Derby aboard Lawring, and he won his first Triple Crown with Whirlaway in 1941.

Arcaro was not happy with the thought of riding Whirlaway in the 1941 Kentucky Derby. Whirlaway's trainer, the legendary "Plain" Ben Jones, persuaded Eddie to take the mount.

"I initially didn't want to ride Whirlaway in the Kentucky Derby," Arcaro said. "But when Ben Jones had me come down and work him out one morning to prove to me that he wouldn't bolt. He sat on his pony at the quarter pole, about four feet off the rail, and told me to go inside of him. I thought he was crazy, but he told me, 'Hell, I'm taking a chance with my life, too.' I said to him, 'Why take a chance with either of our lives? This SOB is going to be rolling. If he hits you, we're both going to be taken out. All he said was, 'Trust me.' "

On the morning of the Derby, ten hours before the race, these were Jones' instructions: "Eddie, I absolutely do not want you to get off with this horse. Actually it would suit me better if you were left at the post on

him. If you can get away badly, that will help. At some part of this race you will be in front. If it's at the sixteenth pole, that's okay, but don't take the lead at the quarter pole, or move up to the front on this horse on the turn. Just sit back there. When you call on him he's going to give it to you."

When Eddie walked down the creaking wooden stairs from the jock's room at Churchill Downs to the paddock, Whirlaway looked beautiful with his coat flaming gold and his tail, reaching nearly to the ground, a lighter hue. Then Arcaro saw it! Jones had taken the left cup off the blinkers so that Whirlaway could see the rail. What a daring move ten minutes before the race! Now it was up to Arcaro to pull it off. And pull it off he did, with an eight length victory of two minutes, one and two-fifths seconds.

Ben Jones later told Grantland Rice, "I always knew Whirlaway was a great horse when ridden the right way. He's been a crazy running horse, but he always had the speed, the heart, and the stamina needed to win. It remained for Eddie Arcaro to give him the perfect ride. Whirlaway has just one great burst of speed and he must come from behind. That's the way Arcaro handled him. His strong hands held Whirlaway in check, and even then the horse got away too soon."

Arcaro

But it remained until the spring of 1948 for Eddie Arcaro to dance with the greatest horse he ever rode, Citation. Eddie recalled, "Man and boy, I had been on fast horses beyond number. But this Citation was a horse apart from anything else I had ridden. His stride was frictionless; his vast speed alarming. You could call on him at any time and, as Ben Jones said of him, 'He could run down any horse that ever breathed.'"

Arcaro continued, "Citation was a particularly handsome horse, although not at all flashy. He possessed a wonderful head and was probably a little above average stature. In addition to everything else, he was intelligent, unlike Whirlaway, who was a slow learner. He knew his business when he got out there on the track. He seemed to have a way of knowing what was demanded of him, and he gave without stint. Riding him was like being on a machine equipped with a throttle. You opened it up and away you went. That was Citation."

Odds are the tricks of fate. Eddie Arcaro never would have ridden Citation, Nashua, Kelso, or so many others had not Ruth, Eddie's wife, been feeling ill on March 5, 1948. Albert Snyder, Citation's regular rider and a friend of Eddie's, suggested that they, trainer C.H. Trotter, and Canadian businessman, Donald Fraser go deep-sea fishing along the Florida Keys for a few days following the Widener Handicap at Hialeah. But Ruth became ill, so Eddie flew home to Long Island. On March 13 their empty boat was located on Rabbit Island, and none of their bodies were ever found.

So Eddie, under dire circumstances, inherited the ride on Citation under Ben and Jimmy Jones, Ben's son and Hall of Fame trainer.

Eddie was afraid of Coaltown, Citation's stable mate. He had a world of speed and ability, and Arcaro was afraid he would steal the Derby on the front end. So he asked Ben Jones the question, "Which do you think is the better horse?"

Without blinking an eye, Jones answered: "Eddie, if I thought Coaltown would win this Derby, you'd be on him."

As the race unfolded, Coaltown was eight lengths on top after an eighth of a mile and four lengths in front as they approached the far turn. Arcaro was scared but then asked Citation for his run. He bounded after his stable mate as if equipped with steel springs in his legs, drew even at the three-sixteenth pole, and won going away by three-and-a-half lengths. The Preakness and Belmont were won even easier, Citation tying Count Fleet's record in the Belmont of two minutes, twenty eight and one-fifth seconds.

Eddie said after the Derby, "The spirit of Albert Snyder rode with me as I guided Citation to his victory. Albert had never ridden in a Derby. This would have been his great day—the chance that few riders ever get in their careers, the opportunity to ride a great horse in a big race. I was thinking, too, of the widow and little daughter in Miami, still clinging to the hope that, miraculously, he would turn up."

Showing the world the kind of men they were, jockey Eddie Arcaro and owner Warren Wright each contributed half the purse of that 1948 Kentucky Derby to Mrs. Snyder. This is the true mark of the champion.

Citation was thoroughbred racing's first career million-dollar earner, and he set the modern-day record for consecutive victories with sixteen. That record was later equaled by two-time Horse of the Year, Cigar, but as Arcaro's wife was quick to point out, "Never broken."

Arcaro rode Citation a total of sixteen times, winning thirteen of his record sixteen consecutive races in 1948. "He was the greatest horse I ever rode," Arcaro said, without hesitation.

After winning the Preakness with Hasty Road in 1955, Arcaro rode Nashua to second behind Swaps in the Kentucky Derby, then won the Preakness and Belmont, neither of which Swaps had entered. That set up a $100,000 winner-take-all match race, and Arcaro rode Nashua to an easy victory. He led in winnings for the fifth and final time with $1,864,796 that year.

Arcaro had his last victory in a Triple Crown race with Fabius, a son of Citation, in the 1956 Preakness. He retired early in 1962, because of bursitis in his right arm. He later served as a television commentator in 24,092 races.

Eddie died on November 14, 1997 at the age of eighty-one at his home in Miami, Florida.

Arcaro was elected to the National Horse Racing Hall of Fame in 1958. He was elected to the National Italian American Sports Hall of Fame in 1978.

Arcaro

International Bowling Museum and Hall of Fame, St. Louis, MO

Andy Varipapa, a bowling legend for six decades, was the pioneer of trick-shot bowling in the United States.

Varipapa was born March 31, 1891, in Carfizza, Italy, and came to America at age twelve. He went on to become one of the most proficient bowlers as well as one of the most popular men in the ten-pin sport of all time.

Andy was so good that he went on to star in the first bowling film short *Strikes and Spares* in 1934 and proceeded to film more trick-shot films than any other bowler.

He performed in exhibitions all over the country and was credited with helping move the sport from

Varipapa

International Bowling Museum and Hall of Fame, St. Louis, MO

Andy Varipapa displays his release.

Varipapa

the rear of barrooms to prominence as one of the most popular competitive sports in America.

Although Andy was considered to be the finest ten-pin bowler in America, he was perhaps better known for his trick shots.

Andy had an amazing list of accomplishments including seventy-eight perfect games, winning numerous bowling titles, terrorizing the competition on the match game circuit, and inventing and performing trick-shots. His most famous stunt was bowling two balls at the same time, crossing them in mid-lane before knocking down the pins.

Charlie Kaplan, who often traveled with Andy, said he never remembered a bowler accepting a money challenge from Andy. "Most of the time they would walk away and say no thanks," said Kaplan.

In 1946 at age fifty-five, Andy won the All-Star Tournament and then repeated in 1947.

While being interviewed on radio, Andy said, "Most of my stunts come to me in my dreams. I always enjoyed trying something new."

In 1946 and 1947, Andy teamed with friend Lou Campi to win the National Double Title.

He was named Bowler of the Year in 1948 and numerous honors would follow. At the age of sixty-eight, Andy won the $6,000 jackpot by tossing nine strikes in a row on Milton Berle's "Jackpot Bowling."

Andy often praised his own workmanship. He was good and was proud to let people know. "If I had been a golfer I would have putted with precision. As a bowler, I am a master of rhythm. That's why Varipapa is so good."

President Richard Nixon invited Varipapa to a White House reception. After shaking hands with Nixon, he claimed, "I could see he didn't have calluses like me. That meant he didn't practice enough. I told him, if he didn't practice more, he wouldn't become a good bowler."

Andy Varipapa died August 25, 1984, in Hempstead, New York. He was inducted into the American Bowling Congress Hall of Fame in 1957 and into the National Italian American Sports Hall of Fame in 1980.

Varipapa

Mosconi

I t is hard to believe that a man who dominated pocket billiards as no one has before or since, winning the World Championship fifteen times from 1941 to 1957, might never have started in the sport if his mother had kept closer count of her potatoes.

But that's the way it was with William Joseph Mosconi, better known as Willie, born in Philadelphia in 1913.

Although Willie's father owned a billiard parlor, he forbade his young son to play, locking up balls and cue sticks at night. He wanted Willie to become a vaudeville star under the tutelage of his uncles, Charles and Louis Mosconi, who were successful dancers.

However, Willie, a reluctant although very good dancing pupil, foiled his father's plans. Late at night,

Willie would sneak in the billiards parlor and practice, using his mother's round potatoes and broomstick for accessories.

One day Uncle Charlie challenged six-year-old Willie to a game, and the youngster ran off fifteen straight balls. Accepting the inevitable, his father began encouraging Willie to play, setting up many exhibition matches. But Willie grew tired of the pace, and "retired" at the age of seven.

Willie graduated from high school in 1931, but had to drop out of college to help support his ailing parents. He worked for a time as an upholsterer's apprentice. On the way home one day after an argument with his foreman, he saw a sign advertising a billiards tournament. He entered, won it, and pocketed seventy-five dollars. His professional career was under way.

Willie first came to prominence in 1933, winning a national divisional tournament in Philadelphia and sectional in New York City before finishing second in the national championships at Minneapolis.

A 112-day tour with world pocket billiards champion Ralph Greenleaf followed. Willie won 50 of the 107 matches. He learned much from Greenleaf, getting most of his wins toward the end of the tour after days of studying Greenleaf in action.

Through 1940, Willie played well in the world championship tournaments, but not quite good enough to win. That changed in 1941 as Willie stormed through to take the title by thirty-two games, including nine games of 125-and-out and fifty runs of 100 or more. Mosconi reigned as world champion fourteen more times before the competition ended after 1957 with Willie on top.

Mosconi, inducted into the Billiard Congress of American Hall of Fame in 1968, and a member of the BCA rules committee, owns many records. Most impressive are the amazing high run of 526 balls, and a high grand average of 18.34 in tournament play.

Except for an Army stint in World War II, Willie kept actively playing in exhibition matches throughout the country. He wrote two books, *Willie Mosconi on Pocket Billiards* and *Winning Pocket Billiards*, and as technical advisor helped prepare Paul Newman and Jackie Gleason for their roles in the movie *The Hustler*.

Mosconi, who headed the Billiard Pro Advisory Staff for Ajay/Ebonite, Delavan, Wisconsin, a Fuqua Sporting Goods Group company, took pride that his many public appearances over the years have helped transform billiards into a family game. "It's now a game that belongs to everybody—young and old, men and women, even kids," he said.

Willie Mosconi died in December 1993, in Haddon Heights, New Jersey. He was survived by his wife Flora and two daughters.

He was elected to the National Italian American Sports Hall of Fame in 1979.

Mosconi

Battalion of Italian Stallions

By Eddie Gold

Joe Pepitone, Doug Buffone, Carmen Fanzone.
Joe Altobelli, Andy Robustelli, Dino Ciccarelli.
The brothers Dom DiMaggio and Vince DiMaggio.
– And a 56-game hitting streak by Joe DiMaggio.

Dante Lavelli, Andy Granatelli, Johnny Antonelli.
Mike Lucci, Bruno Branducci, Johnny Mariucci.
Frankie Crosetti, Vito Valentinetti, Dave Reghetti.
– And a one-handed shot by Hank Luisetti.

Babe Pinelli, Angelo Bertelli, Joe Scibelli.
Carl Furillo, Lennie Merullo, Oscar Melillo.
Billy Conigliaro, Tony Conigliaro, Ed Marinaro.
– And five Kentucky Derby winners by Eddie Arcaro.

Roy Campanella, Johnny Boccabella, Danny Gardella.
Dolph Camilli, Babe Parilli, Lee Mazzilli.
Willie Pastrano, Rocky Graziano, Ron Luciano.
– And one-round knockouts by Rocky Marciano.

Yogi Berra, Primo Carnera, Dale Berra.
Frank Malzone, Rick Cerone, Pete Falcone.
Bill Melchioni, Donna Capponi, Joe Marconi.
– And a pocketful of miracles by Willie Mosconi.

Tony Esposito, Rocky Colavito, Phil Esposito.
Marius Russo, Joe Musso, Rudy LaRusso.
Gino Marchetti, Gary Famiglietti, Gino Cappelletti.
– And a zooming Indy 500 victory by Mario Andretti.

Billy Petrolle, Gino Cimoli, Tim Foli.
Tony Cuccinello, Joey Giardello, Tami Mauriello.
Leo Nomellini, Wash Serini, Bob Avellini.
— AND THE BOOM BOOM FISTS OF RAY MANCINI.

Sibby Sisti, Joe DeMaestri, Ken Silvestri.
Joe Geri, Tony Canzoneri, Tony Lazzeri.
Ernie Lombardi, Vic Lombardi, Wayne Belardi.
— AND THE PACK IS BACK WITH VINCE LOMBARDI.

Phil Rizzuto, Ron Santo, Tony Galento.
Buzz Fazio, Alex Delvecchio, Ed Abbattichio.
John Castino, Dan Marino, Johnny Berardino.
— AND BOWLING 'EM OVER BY CARMEN SALVINO.

Dom Dallessandro, Sal Bando, Bad Boy Orlando.
Joe Garagiola, Darcy Rota, Black Jack Lanza.
Gene Ronzani, Dante Magnani, Lou Nanne.
— AND AN ICY FIGURE-EIGHT BY LINDA FRATIANNE.

Danny Frisella, Al Zarilla.
Gary Gaetti, John Cappelletti, Joe Micheletti.
Al Gionfriddo, Tony Canadeo, Carmen Basilio.
— AND A BROCK-BUSTER TRADE FOR ERNIE BROGLIO.

Steve Durbano, Sam Rutigliano, Joe Pignatano.
Lou Fontinato, Johnny Brocato, Joe Fortunato.
You gotta have that Raging Bull, Jake LaMotta.
— SO THAT FAT LADY CAN SING FOR DICK MOTTA.

Joe DeNucci, Rico Petrocelli, Ralph Raymond.
Steve Palermo, Joe Montana, Tony DeMarco.
— AND A HEISMAN FOR JOE BELLINO.

(Used with permission.)

NATIONAL ITALIAN AMERICAN SPORTS HALL OF FAME INDUCTEES

1977
Sammy Angott
Carmen Basilio
Batt Battalino
Tony Canzoneri
Primo Carnera
Angelo Dundee
Rocky Graziano
Jake LaMotta
Rocky Marciano
Willie Pep

1978
Lou Ambers
Eddie Arcaro
Charles Atlas
Dom DiMaggio
Joe DiMaggio
Tony Lazzeri
Vince Lombardi
Gino Marchetti
Charlie Trippi
Johnny Wilson

1979
Yogi Berra
Tony Canadeo
Phil Cavarretta
Buttercup Dickerson
Joey Giardello
Ernie Lombardi
Hank Luisetti
Joey Maxim

Willie Mosconi
Leo Nomellini
Gene Sarazen

1980
Ed Abbatticcio
Ping Bodie
Peter DePaolo
Andy Granatelli
Hank Marino
Brian Piccolo
Phil Rizzuto
Andy Robustelli
Andy Varipapa

1981
Mario Andretti
Donna Caponi
Rocky Colavito
Tony DeMarco
Ralph DePalma
Phil Esposito
Fidel LaBarba
Dante Lavelli

1982
Alan Ameche
Frank Carideo
Young Corbett III
Alex Delvecchio
Red DiBernardi
Sal Maglie
George Musso

1983
Franco Columbu
Tony Conigliaro
Buzz Fazio
Vincent Pazzetti
Ron Santo
Ken Venturi

1984
Angelo Bertelli
Gino Cappelletti
Frank Crosetti
Lou Little
Gus Mancuso
Sammy Mandell
Joe Torre

1985–1986
Nick Buoniconti
Frank Coltiletti
Chet Forte
Linda Frattiane
Carl Furillo
Pete Herman
Carmen Salvino

1987
Tony Esposito
Frankie Genaro
Daryl Lamonica
Joe Paterno
Vic Rascbi

1988

Ben Abruzzo
Ray Barbuti
Joe Bellino
Zeke Bonura
Giorgio Chinaglia
Joe Garagiola
Franco Harris
Harry Jeffra
John Mariucci
Kelly Petillo

1989

Gene Brito
John Cappelletti
Harry Caray
Frank DeMaree
Vince DiMaggio
Ted Hendricks
Anges Iori-Robertson
Tom Lasorda
Johnny Petraglia
Bruno Sammartino

1990–1991

Dolph Camilli
Roy Campanella
Al Cervi
Tony Cuccinello
Joe Fortunato
Marty Liquori
Billy Martin
Phil Villapiano

1992–1993

Matt Biondi
Doug Buffone
Doug Ford
Bartlett Giamatti
Mary Lou Retton

1994

Lou Campi
Jerry Colangelo
Lou Ferrigno
Ray Mancini
Ed Marinaro
Rico Petrocelli
Richard Ruffalo
Tony Sacco

1995

Sal Bando
Mike Lucci
Greg Mannino
Susan Notorangelo
John Panelli

1996–1997

Joey Amalfitano
Brian Boitano
Lou Carnesecca
Lou Duva
Joe Montana
Lewa "Rocco" Yacilla

1998

Gary Beban
Santo Catanzaro

Chip Ganassi
Tony LaRussa

1999

Ernie Di Gregorio
Mike Eruzione
Jim Fregosi
Harry Pezzullo
Rick Pitino
Paul Tagliabue

2000

Dan Baisone
Mark Bavaro
Larry Brignolia
Dino Ciccarelli
Eleanor Garatti
Rollie Massimino
Babe Pinelli
Lindy Remigino
Jimmy Smith

2001

Joe Amato
Peter Cutino
Vince Ferragamo
Dr. Donna Lopiano
Dick Vitale

2002

Michael Andretti
Michael Bolletteri
Mike DiCiccio

ACKNOWLEDGEMENTS

The author was aided considerably by the available *Book on Sports*, and is especially grateful to Tim Cohane's *Great College Football Coaches*. The author wishes to thank: the National Italian American Sports Hall of Fame, International Boxing Hall of Fame, Pro Football Hall of Fame, Naismith Memorial Basketball Hall of Fame, National Baseball Hall of Fame, International Bowling Hall of Fame, and International Gymnastics all of Fame for their courtesy and assistance. Also the sports information offices of:

- Boston Bruins
- Boston Red Sox
- Boston University
- Los Angeles Dodgers
- Manhattan College
- Miami Dolphins
- New England Patriots
- New York Jets
- New York Yankees
- Notre Dame University
- Pennsylvania State University
- San Francisco 49ers
- St. John's University
- Stanford University
- University of Miami
- United States Naval Academy
- Wisconsin University

I wish also to thank for their assistance: Tim Cohane, Everett Skehan, Eddie Gold, former sports writer for the *Chicago Sun Times*, WGNTV–Chicago, Steve Morris, Paul Daly, Barbara Figurski, Kathryn, Katie, and Jena Beauregard, Steve Phillips, Bob Hampton, G.F. Williams, Roger Bennett, Alan Powers, Jim Cunavelis, and John Vanesse.

In addition, the following organizations were extremely helpful:

Downtown Athletic Club, Worcester Public Library, *The Worcester Telegram & Gazette*, Smithsonian Institution, Jimmy Burchfield's Classic Entertainment and Sports Company, U.S.A. Softball, and Kevin Huard's Yesterdays Legends.